Designing Positive Behavior Support Plans

SECOND EDITION

Linda M. Bambara | **Timothy P. Knoster**

American Association
on Intellectual and
Developmental Disabilities

Copyright © 2009 by Linda M. Bambara and Timothy P. Knoster

Published by
American Association on Intellectual and Developmental Disabilities
501 3rd Street, NW, Suite 200
Washington, DC 20001-2760

The points of view herein are those of the authors and do not necessarily represent the
official policy or opinion of the American Association on Intellectual and Developmental
Disabilities. Publication does not imply endorsement by the editor, the Association, or its
individual members.

Printed in the United States of America.

Library of Congress Cataloging-in-Publication Data

Bambara, Linda M., 1952–
    Designing positive behavior support plans / Linda M. Bambara, Tim Knoster.—
2nd ed.
        p. cm.
    Includes bibliographical references.
    ISBN 978-1-935304-03-6
1. Behavior modification—United States. 2. Children with mental
disabilities—Education—United States. 3. Problem
children—Education—United States. I. Knoster, Tim, 1956– II. Title.
    LB1060.2.B35 2009
      371.92—dc22

                        2009013490

Contents

CHAPTER 1

What Is Positive Behavior Support?

Tasha throws her building blocks at children in her preschool classroom. For no apparent reason, Johnny constantly pushes and scratches other kindergartners on the playground. On an unpredictable basis Kelly falls kicking and screaming onto the hallway floor when moving with her third-grade classmates from one room to another. David slaps his face with his hands whenever the staff at the middle school asks him to perform any type of task. Julia's offensive language and inappropriate touching is creating a serious problem in her job and community.

Chances are you know a student whose problem behavior is as difficult as Tasha's, Johnny's, Kelly's, David's, or Julia's. If you are confused about why these problems exist and what to do to make the situation better, you are not alone!

Challenge Gives Rise to Innovation

Students with disabilities who engage in serious problem behavior present us with some of our greatest challenges. Conventional approaches to "manage" such problems are often ineffective, primarily for two reasons. First, the common application of behavior management has paid little attention to understanding (a) who the person is, (b) what the social contexts for the behavior are, and (c) what the function or purpose of the problem behavior is. Second, conventional management procedures have placed exclusive emphasis on using negative consequences to suppress or control the person's behavior, rather than teaching and reinforcing socially appropriate alternative skills. Conventional approaches often fail because they ignore the underlying influences for problem behaviors. As long as the conditions that contribute to a student's problem behaviors continue to exist, the individual will be motivated to use problem behaviors to get his or her needs met. This is often the case for many students with intellectual disabilities who have a limited repertoire of social problem-solving skills.

PBS Defined

Positive behavior support (PBS), a more effective alternative, is a problem-solving approach that student-centered teams can use to understand and then address environmental factors that contribute to a student's use of problem behaviors. Rather than exclusively using consequences to control inappropriate behaviors, PBS emphasizes prevention, or changing problem environments, and teaching so that the student learns alternative means for addressing his needs. The ultimate goal of PBS is to help individuals with a history of engaging in challenging behaviors achieve a quality life. PBS is also empirically driven. PBS builds on research-based practices shown to be effective for many different individuals and problem behaviors in school, home, and community settings. Further, because PBS uses data to document effectiveness with each individual student, its validity is documented again and again with each application.

PBS in Schools

When PBS first emerged, the focus was almost exclusively on individual students who presented serious behavioral challenges (e.g., Tasha, Johnny, Kelly, David, Julia). More recently, the basic principles of PBS have been applied systemically to entire schools so that all students can benefit. When PBS is applied to a whole school context, it is known as schoolwide positive behavior support, or SWPBS.

• •

Schoolwide PBS is an approach to school discipline that incorporates specific practices and systems designed to produce socially important and sustained improvement in the behavioral culture of a school.

—Horner, Sugai, Todd, & Lewis-Palmer, 2005, p. 383

SWPBS consists of a continuum of three levels of intervention that vary in intensity based on student needs. *Primary prevention (or universal strategies)* targets all students in a school building. The focus of this level of intervention is to prevent problem behaviors for most students in the general school population by implementing schoolwide preventive practices that emphasize establishing and teaching appropriate, acceptable behaviors. Posting and teaching schoolwide expectations for positive social behaviors and rewarding expected behaviors are examples of primary prevention strategies.

Secondary prevention provides group-based interventions for students who are not sufficiently responsive to primary prevention, but for whom intensive, individualized interventions may be unnecessary. The students targeted for this level of intervention are generally considered at risk for pervasive behavioral challenges if their needs go unaddressed over time. Some examples of strategies at this level include group social skills training that focuses on conflict resolution, anger management, or social problem solving, as well as mentoring programs.

Tertiary prevention, also known as *individualized PBS,* consists of highly individualized behavior supports for students who present pervasive or persistent behavioral challenges. Typically students who require individualized supports are not sufficiently responsive to the first two levels of prevention. These students often require specialized interventions and supports that are uniquely tailored to their circumstances and learning needs. This book specifically focuses on this tertiary level of PBS supports for students with intellectual and other developmental disabilities. Figure 1 presents some considerations for when an individualized positive behavior support plan may be needed.

FIGURE 1

Considerations for Determining When Individualized PBS Is Needed

An individualized positive behavior support plan is needed in the following cases:

- The child's challenging behavior persists despite consistently implemented classroom-based interventions.

- The child's behavior places the child or others at risk of (a) harm or injury and/or (b) exclusion and devaluation (e.g., suspension/expulsion).

- School personnel are considering more intrusive and restrictive procedures, and/or a more restrictive placement for the child.

PBS interventions are considered state of the art by many experts and have resulted in widespread use in schools across the United States. PBS employs research-based practices that have been shown to produce positive outcomes for students through formal research studies. Currently, PBS at all three levels of intervention enjoys strong empirical support, which is continually emerging (see Safran & Oswald, 2003, quoted below). In addition, the Individuals with Disabilities Education Improvement Act (IDEA) of 2004 contains specific language that supports the use of PBS practices in schools for students with disabilities (see Figure 2). In the next section we describe the guiding principles and key features of PBS at the individual student, or tertiary, level of support.

● ●

Overall, research has shown that the use of PBS at
all three levels of intervention, primary, secondary, and tertiary
(individual) prevention, has consistently yielded positive effects
for students with and without disabilities.

—Safran & Oswald, 2003

FIGURE 2
IDEA Provisions for Positive Behavior Support

IDEA 2004 supports the use of positive behavior support in the following ways. IDEA indicates the following:

- In cases in which a behavioral intervention plan is needed (i.e., when a child's behavior impedes his or her learning or that of others), the Individualized Education Program (IEP) team shall consider, when appropriate, strategies, including *positive behavioral interventions,* to address the child's behavior.

- As a member of the IEP team, the regular education teacher, along with other members of the IEP, shall participate in the development of the IEP, including giving consideration to *positive behavioral interventions* to address behaviors that interfere with learning.

- In cases in which a severe disciplinary action is being considered resulting in a change of placement such as suspension from school, the IEP shall convene to conduct a *functional behavior assessment* and implement a behavior intervention plan where the team finds the conduct in question substantially related to the child's disability. This must be done within 10 school days of any decision to change a placement of a child. In situations in which a behavior intervention has been developed, the team should modify it as necessary.

Guiding Principles

Positive behavior support is guided by basic principles or assumptions about behaviors and, more specifically, effective interventions.

First, challenging behaviors are context related. Challenging behaviors are triggered and maintained by something in the person's environment. This principle asserts that problem behaviors do not occur randomly, or for "no reason at all," but are governed by the conditions under which they occur. When challenging behaviors do occur, they signal that something in the prevailing environment is disturbing or provoking to the individual.

Environmental influences may be discrete events external or internal to the individual, such as being presented with a difficult work task, being told what to do, having a bad cold, or feeling very tired. Environmental influences may also be broad and consist of an interplay of multiple factors. One's daily routines, quality of social relationships, experiences with negative events, and lack of opportunity to participate in personally meaningful activities—all may have a significant impact on the display of challenging behaviors.

Challenging behaviors are not caused by a person's disability. People do not engage in self-stimulation because of autism or engage in aggressive acts because of an intellectual disability. It is true, however, that each person's abilities and characteristics often determine how one responds to environmental circumstances. For example, some individuals can easily handle a change in routine, while others who prefer consistency can become quite upset, screaming and crying in response to the simplest change. It is the change in routine, not the person's disability, that provokes the problem behavior. In short, challenging behaviors occur for a reason; they are related to the context in which they occur.

Second, challenging behaviors serve a function for the student. Although socially unacceptable, and at times even dangerous, students engage in problem behaviors because they serve a useful purpose from the perspective of the student. Although students may not be fully aware of how they may be impacting their environment through problem behaviors, problem behaviors nonetheless work to get their needs addressed. Students may engage in problem behavior to escape or avoid unpleasant situations, or to gain access to desired activities, objects, or social interactions. Another way to say this is that problem behaviors are communicative. That is, the purpose of problem behavior is to bring about a social change; problem behaviors communicate that the student may be seeking to avoid unpleasant events (e.g., "I don't want to do this") or to gain access to desired events (e.g., "I want this").

Positive behavior support assumes that students with developmental disabilities often engage in problem behaviors because they have not acquired socially acceptable responses that work as well as the problem behaviors for achieving desired outcomes. For example, for a child with limited communication skills, falling to the floor can communicate quite clearly that he does not want to go to the next activity. In some cases where the student has alternative means of communicating, the way we respond to the student's communicative attempts may inadvertently foster problem behaviors, rather than encourage positive alternatives. For example, we may listen and respond to the student's problem behavior (e.g., falling to the floor) while ignoring other more socially appropriate messages such as the statement, "I don't want to play kickball in the gym." In either case, teaching alternative skills becomes the central focus of positive behavior support.

Third, effective interventions are based on a thorough understanding of the student, his or her social contexts, and the function of the problem behavior. Current research suggests that the most effective interventions are assessment based and directly linked to known environmental influences and to the function of the problem behavior. Once the function of the challenging behavior is understood, the goal is to teach socially acceptable alternatives. Once environmental influences are understood, the goal is to (a) modify these variables to minimize disturbing situations for the individual, (b) prevent problem behaviors from occurring, and (c) encourage the student's long-term use of alternative skills. These three goals contribute to the long-term effectiveness of positive behavior support plans.

• •

The most effective individualized interventions are based on assessment-based hypotheses that explain why problem behavior is occurring.

—Carr et al., 1999

Fourth, positive behavior support must be grounded in person-centered values that respect the dignity, preferences, and goals of each student. More than a technology to reduce problem behavior, positive behavior support is grounded in person-centered values that treat all people, regardless of their level of ability or the nature of their challenging behavior, with the same respect and dignity we hold for ourselves. This means that interventions must not stigmatize people with disabilities and must be acceptable for same-age peers without disabilities in typical settings.

Person-centered values also require us to honor personal preferences and goals and to work toward outcomes that are not just important to teachers and parents, but are also meaningful to the students themselves. Positive behavior support facilitates opportunities, such as friendships, improved social relationships, participation in typical school and community activities, and access to a variety of preferred events, that might otherwise be denied to students who engage in problem behavior. Lifestyle enhancement in inclusive settings is a central feature of positive behavior support. It is both the necessary context for and goal of intervention effectiveness.

Characteristics

Based on these four principles, individualized PBS is characterized by a comprehensive, values-based approach for addressing the unique needs of people who engage in challenging behaviors. PBS is a problem-solving process in which a team of people most familiar with the student seek to first understand the reasons for the problem behavior and then select interventions and supports designed to address the student's needs. The problem-solving process begins with a functional assessment in which we identify the environmental influences and the function or purpose of the challenging behaviors, along with individual student strengths, preferences, and interests. We then customize the behavior support plan to address the student's individual needs and life circumstances; plans consist of multiple interventions or support strategies that emphasize alternative skill training, environmental adaptations, and long-term supports. The goal of positive behavior support is to achieve long-lasting, meaningful results. Success in this regard is measured not only in terms of reductions in problem behaviors, but also by increases in the performance of alternative skills and improvements in the person's quality of life. Key characteristics of individualized PBS are listed in Table 1.

T A B L E 1
Characteristics of Individualized PBS

- PBS is a problem-solving process for addressing the support needs of individual students who engage in problem behaviors.

- PBS is team based; it involves those familiar with the student in the planning and decision making.

- PBS is assessment based. Interventions and supports are directly linked to environmental influences and hypotheses concerning the function of the student's problem behavior.

- PBS plans are comprehensive, usually involving multiple interventions and supports. (Rarely is only one strategy adequate.)

- PBS is proactive, emphasizing prevention, by changing the environment and teaching alternative skills.

- PBS emphasizes lifestyle enhancement in inclusive settings.

- PBS is person centered; it honors the dignity and preferences of the individual student.

- PBS is designed for use in everyday settings using typically available resources.

- PBS holds a broad view of success that includes (a) increases in the use of alternative skills, (b) decreases in the incidence of problem behavior, and (c) improvements in quality of life.

Collaboration and Teaming

Why Team?

Designing a comprehensive behavior support plan requires a collaborative team approach. Teams generate solutions to problems, share resources and information, work together to implement behavior supports across settings, and assure mutual accountability for success. Collaborative teaming is important for several reasons.

A team approach can

- bring together different ideas and perspectives about the student and the student's problem behavior for a comprehensive understanding;

- foster consensus building, as well as shared responsibility and accountability across team members;

- help team members select effective and practical interventions and supports that can realistically be carried out in typical classroom, home, or community settings;

- provide an ongoing source of support for all team members.

In essence, when team members work together and collaborate on solutions to problems the quality and effectiveness of a student's behavior support plan is enhanced. Working together is especially important when a student engages in problem behaviors across settings and when multiple providers (e.g., teachers, therapists, paraeducators) are involved in the student's support. No one person holds the best understanding of the student or knowledge of what might work in all situations. Sustainability of a support plan is also enhanced through collaborative teaming because once team members come to a common understanding of the student's problem behaviors, they can then agree on how to best implement interventions and supports across settings and within the resources of the team. In fact, given the complexity of some students' problem behaviors, effective supports may be impossible without collaboration among key players.

Teaming can provide an important source of support for team members as well. Let's face it. Supporting students with behavioral challenges is not easy. Camaraderie, shared decision making, and learning from others' successes and frustrations can support team members to persist through times of difficulty. Ultimately the student benefits when team members feel supported.

School personnel and parents report that collaborative teaming provides an important source of support to PBS team members. Teaming greatly assists team members to learn new skills and sustain their efforts during times of difficulty.

—Bambara, Nonnemacher, & Kern, in press

Who should be on a student-centered team? Team composition varies according to student needs, but should include (a) people who know the student well or have a vested interest in participating (e.g., family members, the student where appropriate), (b) people who have the expertise to help team members make good decisions (e.g., school administrators, behavior support specialists, school psychologists, caseworkers), and (c) people who are likely to carry out behavior supports on a daily basis (e.g., teachers, paraeducators). Despite the practical challenges of forging working partnerships with families in school settings, parents or other family members should be involved in the team. Not only can parents share critical information about the student with the team, but they are likely to be vested in the process as they, along with their son or daughter, will live with the results. Their involvement also can help to ensure the continuity of supports across the years as a student transitions across classrooms and teachers. Furthermore, by ensuring that parents are active members of a team, families are supported to try new strategies at home that complement school interventions. In the long run, parent involvement can greatly enhance positive outcomes for the student.

Organizing School Teams

Effective teams meet regularly. Yet finding the time to meet is a common struggle for school teams. Schools that have been successful with implementing student-centered teams create opportunities for teaming within the school organization. Some of the best team configurations infuse PBS practices within existing school teams that have a process in place for meeting regularly and considering individual student needs. For example, PBS teaming practices can be implemented within a school's instructional or student assistance teams or within grade level teams.

Where there are no standing school teams, creating a working group from the student's IEP team is a logical choice. Regardless of how teams are developed, however, all student-centered teams should involve key players in the student's life. Standing teams will need to be reconfigured to include those who interact with the student daily.

Some students may have many professionals involved in their lives. In such cases when a team is large, it may be helpful to identify a core team, or a subset of an extended team, whose members meet regularly to design the student's behavior support plan. Working within a smaller group can help make meetings more time efficient and easier to arrange. The core team typically includes those with the most relevant expertise and frequent dealings with the student (e.g., parents, teachers, paraeducators, behavior specialists). The core team can then pull in other extended team members for their particular expertise or for periodic updates as needed.

Team Role and Process
No one behavior support plan will work for all students, and no one intervention is best for any given individual. Once the reasons for a problem behavior are understood, the team usually has many different intervention and support options to consider. To be effective in the long run, teams must select support options that best address student needs, have a "good fit" within everyday routines and environments, and can be realistically carried out by team members.

· ·

A support plan has a "good contextual fit" when it (a) is responsive to the goals and values of team members; (b) makes use of the knowledge and experiences of the team; and (c) is compatible with typical activities and routines in school, home, and community settings. A good contextual fit is likely to increase consumer satisfaction, as well as contribute to long-term success.

—Albin, Lucyshyn, Horner, & Flannery, 1996

TABLE 2
Team Decisions and Actions

PBS steps	Team actions
Functional assessment	▪ Prioritize and define targeted problem behaviors ▪ Decide on what information to gather ▪ Decide on how and who gathers information ▪ Analyze and interpret gathered information ▪ Come to consensus on hypotheses for problem behaviors
Design and implement behavior support plan	▪ Brainstorm and consider intervention options based on hypotheses for problem behavior across all PBS intervention components ▪ Select options matched to student needs and team resources ▪ Develop action plan for implementing
Evaluate and monitor PBS outcomes	▪ Determine outcomes to measure ▪ Decide on ways to measure outcomes and progress ▪ Determine whether the support plan is working ▪ Modify plan as needed

The role of the team is to engage in shared decision making throughout the steps of the PBS process: functional assessment, designing a positive behavior support plan, and evaluating and monitoring progress. Table 2 (above) summarizes key decision-making actions that teams will make at each step of this process. These actions are described in more detail in the subsequent chapters of this book.

To make shared decisions, teams will follow some variation of a problem-solving approach. Typically, this problem solving consists of the team

▪ identifying the problem to be solved (the guiding questions posed throughout this book can help teams clarify the problem);

- brainstorming ideas or solutions to the problem;

- discussing pros and cons of proposed solutions;

- selecting options that best fit the student's and the team's needs;

- making an action plan to implement selected options;

- monitoring and evaluating PBS outcomes.

All team members lend their expertise to the problem-solving process. To be maximally effective, one team member may take on a leadership role coordinating team activities and walking other members through the decision-making process. Team leaders often have dual expertise in PBS and in facilitating team collaboration (e.g., establishing expectations and open communication, resolving conflicts, encouraging accountability).

Purpose and Organization of This Book

The purpose of this book is to provide a conceptual framework for understanding, designing, and evaluating positive behavior support plans for individual students with developmental disabilities who require comprehensive behavioral supports. From our perspective, designing positive behavior supports is more of a way of thinking about how to approach problems than it is about specific assessment or particular intervention strategies. Toward this end, our goal is to provide a concise reference guide for student-centered school teams to use as they think through the process. Critical questions are offered throughout the book to guide team decision making. This book is best used in conjunction with other resources identified in the Resource Bibliography (Appendix E) for teams seeking more specific assessment and intervention information.

Although our focus is designing individualized PBS plans in schools, the process we lay out is relevant for people with developmental disabilities across different age ranges and settings. Parents and community service providers will find this information useful as well for designing in-home and other community-based supports. In fact, the process we describe for developing behavior support plans is relevant for individuals with other types of disabilities or no disabilities at all.

Designing a positive behavior support plan begins with an understanding of the student. In chapter 2 we overview the functional assessment process by highlighting the steps for gathering important informa- tion and generating hypotheses about the nature of the problem behavior. In chapter 3 we provide  guidelines for developing a comprehensive, assessment-based support plan involving four primary intervention components: (a) short-term prevention in the form of antecedent and setting-event modifications, (b) teaching alternative skills, (c) consequence interventions (including crisis intervention), and (d) long-term prevention strategies. Chapter 4 provides considerations for evaluating the success of a support plan. In chapter 5 we address some practical considerations and discuss ways in which teams can abridge the process to address pressing student needs and team concerns through early intervention. Finally, the book includes appendixes that contain examples of complete support plans for two students and informational resources on designing individualized supports.

CHAPTER 2

Begin With an Understanding: The Functional Assessment Process

Elena, a 7-year-old diagnosed with severe intellectual disabilities and autism, receives special education services at her local elementary school. It's 1:30 p.m., time for free play on the school playground, one of the few periods during which the playground is available for Elena's class. Elena's classmates are dispersed among two third-grade classes throughout the playground area. Roberto and Rachel are on the swings, giggling as the teacher's assistant pushes them higher and higher. Mrs. Gallago helps Jonathan climb the slide. Michael spins on the tire swing, while Maria sits in the sandbox sifting sand through her fingertips, enjoying the warm sun.

Elena paces alone in the middle of the playground. "I'll give you a turn on the swing in just a minute," the teacher assistant calls out. Suddenly Elena's pacing picks up speed. She darts back and forth between the swing set and the sandbox, flapping her hands as she changes direction. No one seems to notice. Elena lets out a loud shriek. Familiar with Elena's signal, her teachers immediately look up but "do not attend," hoping that Elena will calm herself. Elena's screaming intensifies as she jumps up and down. The teachers maintain a watchful eye. "You'll get your turn soon," the assistant shouts out, hoping to appease Elena. Elena slaps her face hard. She falls screaming and proceeds rhythmically to bang her forehead on the playground turf.

The teachers rush to her side. They can no longer ignore her behavior. Mrs. Gallago cradles Elena in her arms, talking to her softly as she prevents Elena from further self-injury. As Mrs. Gallago looks up, she notices that the third-graders have stopped their activity, watching the scene from around the playground. I have to do something, Mrs. Gallago says to herself. This is the seventh episode today. I counted at least 20 times this week. Where do I begin? What should I do?

Ask Why

Before asking yourself the obvious question, What can I do? start by asking, Why? Why is the student engaging in problem behavior? What conditions, specific situations, or triggers appear to be contributing to the problem? What purpose does the problem behavior serve for the person? Could the student be using problem behavior to communicate specific messages?

Asking why is critical because the effectiveness of any behavioral intervention typically depends on how well it addresses the underlying reasons for problem behavior. Unfortunately, when faced with behavioral challenges, we often ask shortsighted questions. For example, instead of "Why?" we might ask, "What can I do to stop John's aggression? What do you do to stop Karena's food obsessions? How can I get Caitlyn to stop her self-stimulation? What's the best way to handle Andrew's refusal to participate in activities?" These questions are shortsighted because they focus exclusively on the topography, or form, of behavior, rather than on the environmental influences or function of problem behavior. An important rule to keep in mind is that there is no one best intervention that is effective for certain forms of problem behaviors like the ones identified above. Although the topography of a problem behavior may look similar from student to student, the reasons for the problem behavior can be quite varied. For example, some students may hit others (aggression) when they observe a peer receiving teacher praise; some may hit when they encounter a difficult work task or when they are told to do something they do not like; while others may hit when they are bored or lonely. Similarly, the purpose or function of problem behavior may vary although the form of behavior looks the same. Some may hit to avoid a difficult or disliked activity; some may hit to initiate peer or teacher interaction; others may hit to get others to change an activity. Despite the fact that the problem behavior (e.g., hitting) might look the same, the same intervention is not likely to work for all students because the reasons for the problem behavior differ. The most effective course of action is to first understand the reasons for the problem behavior, and then, second, select interventions to address them directly. This can only be accomplished by asking, "Why?"

Functional Assessment

Understanding why an individual engages in challenging behavior generally requires a *functional assessment* or *functional behavioral assessment* (FBA) as identified by IDEA 2004. Functional assessment is a process that involves gathering and analyzing both broad and specific contextual information (e.g., environmental influences) in an effort to explain specific reasons for the student's problem behavior in terms of "triggers" (what sets off problem behaviors) and the purpose or function served by the behavior. During the functional assessment process you and your team will make decisions about (a) what type of information should be gathered, (b) how to gather information (i.e., what assessment tools to use), and (c) who should be involved in gathering information. Once information has been collected, the team synthesizes and interprets the data to identify the reasons for a student's problem behavior. By the end of the assessment process, teams develop hypothesis statements that (a) serve to summarize assessment results, (b) offer explanations for the individual's problem behavior, and (c) guide the development of behavior support plans.

When should you conduct a functional assessment? A functional assessment should always be conducted whenever a team decides that an individualized behavior support plan is needed for a student. IDEA 2004 requires a FBA when, due to problem behavior, a student is removed from his or her current placement for more than 10 consecutive school days. This requirement is a minimum standard. To be maximally effective and proactive, teams should not wait until the student is in crisis or is approaching the 10 consecutive day threshold, but rather should conduct a functional assessment whenever an individualized behavior support plan is needed.

Although conducting a functional assessment does take time, it does not have to be a lengthy process. The amount of time required to gather sufficient information depends on any number of factors, including how well you and your team know the student, how much information you wish to gather, how familiar you are with the tools for gathering information, and how readily you and your team can identify patterns that explain problem behaviors from the information gathered. The point is that functional assessment is a process. The amount of time involved and the comprehensiveness of the assessment will depend on the needs of the student, including the complexity of the problem behavior and the resources and expertise of your team.

Chapter purpose. The purpose of this chapter is to overview the process involved in conducting a comprehensive functional assessment. However, there may be times when a comprehensive functional assessment is not needed. (See chapter 5 for ways and appropriate times to abridge the process.) There are many excellent sources on how to conduct a functional assessment; several are listed in the Resource Bibliography (Appendix E) of this book. We encourage you to become familiar with them. Our goal here is not to detail the process found in other sources, but to outline the basic steps involved. These include (a) prioritize and define the problem behavior, (b) gather a broad array of information, (c) gather specific information, and (c) generate hypothesis statements. We end the chapter with a discussion on tools and sources for conducting a functional assessment.

Prioritize and Define Problem Behavior

The first step in the functional assessment process is to prioritize and define the student's problem behavior(s) that are targeted for intervention. Because students who challenge us often present more than one problem behavior, teams often need to decide which problem behavior(s) to intervene on first, and then define the targeted behaviors so that the problem is clearly identified and observable to all members of the team. In this step, you and your team will ask two important questions.

First, ask, *What problem behaviors are most important to address first?* Prioritizing problem behaviors for intervention is critical; addressing multiple problem behaviors all at once might be too difficult for a team (and the student) to address. To prioritize, consider targeting one or two of the problem behaviors that have the greatest negative impact on the student's learning and participation in typical school, home, or community activities. Priority consideration should be given to behaviors that are destructive (those that are harmful or life or health threatening to the student or others), followed by disruptive behaviors (behaviors that interfere with the student's or others' learning, disrupt daily routines, or prevent the student from participating in typical school, home, or community activities). Distracting behaviors, those that are socially stigmatizing, can be important targets but are lesser priorities for change than the first two types.

Second, ask, *How can problem behaviors be clearly defined?* Once problem behaviors are prioritized and targeted for intervention, define them in observable terms. In other words, define problem behaviors by what you can see the student do. This requires that general terms used to describe problem behaviors, such as aggression, refusals, noncompliance, and self-stimulation, be translated into the behaviors the student actually exhibits. The most direct way to do this is to simply ask, What does the student look and/or sound like when exhibiting problem behavior? Some examples of general terms translated into observable student actions are provided below.

- *Aggression:* Threatening with a raised fist or hitting others.

- *Refusals:* Falling to the floor or sitting with arms crossed.

- *Noncompliance:* Saying "No" or screaming "I hate you" when asked to do something.

- *Self-stimulation:* Rocking back and forth and flapping hands.

Defining problem behaviors in observable terms is an essential step. It helps all team members clearly identify which problem behaviors are targeted for intervention and which will be evaluated during the functional assessment process and then later monitored for change once a support plan has been implemented.

One important note: Sometimes different forms of problem behaviors occur together around related incidents. For example, Jeremy refuses to work by folding his arms, putting his head down on his desk, singing, and then often getting out of his seat and crawling on the floor. In cases like this, when different forms of problem behaviors cluster together around similar incidents, treat them as a single problem behavior but be sure to describe all forms in your definition. When behaviors cluster together they typically serve the same function.

Gather Broad Information

The next step in the functional assessment process is to gather broad contextual information about the student: strengths and skill limitations; preferences, interests, and goals; general health; educational and general history; and overall aspects of quality of life. Although many of these broad contextual influences on problem behavior may be well beyond a team's control, gathering this information is vital to developing comprehensive support plans uniquely tailored to the individual's preferences, needs, and life circumstances. Support plans should result in an improved quality of life for the person, not just a reduction in problem behaviors. At the very least, gathering broad information can sensitize team members to the student's current situation and provide a contextual understanding for how and why problem behaviors developed. This step is especially important for teams whose members do not know the student well or are not thoroughly familiar with the student's abilities and background.

Table 3 lists several important areas of assessment for gathering broad information. Teams need not consider all areas, but should select those that are most relevant to the student. When gathering information in relevant areas, consider how negative factors or student limitations might be contributing to the problem behavior. Conversely, also consider how you can use positive assets or student qualities in each area to strengthen supports for the student.

For example, under student strengths and skill limitations, teams could consider how specific deficits in communication and social skills, such as the student having no symbolic system of communication, might be contributing to problem behavior. Teams can also ask, How does the person communicate currently, and how might these skills be improved

TABLE 3
Gather Broad Information

Assess what areas?

- Student strengths and skill limitations

    Communication skills

    Social skills

    Academic skills

    Problem-solving skills

- Student (including family) interests, preferences, and goals
- General health
- Education and general history
- Quality of life

    Relationships

    Happiness

    Choice and control

    Access to preferred events

    School and community inclusion

Ask

- How do negative factors or student deficits in these areas contribute to problem behavior?
- How can positive assets in these areas be used to strengthen student supports?

as alternatives to problem behaviors? In this area teams might also consider how the student's academic functioning is related to problem behavior. Could the student be "acting out" because the academic work is too difficult? Conversely, how can we build on the student's academic strengths to make undesirable activities more meaningful from the student's perspective?

When assessing a student's interests, preferences, and goals, determine what the student enjoys and consider whether daily school and home routines provide sufficient opportunities for the individual to pursue interests and participate in preferred activities. As a guide, individuals rarely resort to problem behaviors when they are engaged in activities they like. Conversely, consider whether the student's day is filled with events that are disliked, problematic, or particularly stressful. Is the day filled with more disliked than liked activities? Could these negative factors be contributing to the individual's problem behavior?

Under general health, consider whether problem behaviors are related to illness or pain (e.g., a cold, menstrual cramps, chronic anemia), vision or hearing problems, poor dietary or sleep habits, or mental health issues (e.g., depression, anxiety disorder). In addition, because many students with disabilities, particularly those with autism, have sensory integration problems, consider whether problem behaviors may be related to hyper- or hyposensitivity to environmental stimuli. Ultimately you and your team will need to decide whether additional medical/therapeutic evaluations or interventions are required and how you can make accommodations to address the student's health needs (e.g., lessen classroom demands on days when the student has not slept well, avoid art activities that require "messy" hands for a child who is hypersensitive to touch).

With regard to student history, consider whether the student has recently experienced a major life event (e.g., abuse, parent divorce, death, family move, school transfer), especially when problem behavior seems to have suddenly emerged. Gather information on the student's educational history, particularly around educational placements and successful and unsuccessful interventions. Learning about what behavioral interventions worked or did not work in the past can provide important clues about the history of problem behavior.

Finally, gather information about the student's overall lifestyle. What is the quality of the student's relationship with peers and family members? Does the individual seem happy or at least content? Does the person have age-appropriate opportunities for choice and control within daily routines? Does the individual have sufficient access to preferred activities? Is the person included in typical school and community activities? Answers to such questions not only provide significant clues for understanding what factors appear to be contributing to the problem behavior, but also help to identify relevant goals for the person's support plan.

Gather Specific Information

In this third step of the functional assessment process, teams gather specific information that will (a) pinpoint the conditions that are regularly associated with the problem behavior and (b) identify the function or purpose of the individual's behavior. This step typically requires direct observation of the student during typical activities and records of the occurrence of problem behaviors. Observations continue usually over the course of several days until predicable patterns emerge around four key questions. Table 4 lists these four important questions.

T A B L E 4
Gather Specific Information

Questions to answer

1. When and in what activities is the student most likely to engage in problem behavior?

2. What specific antecedent or setting events are most likely to trigger problem behavior?

3. What function(s) does the problem behavior serve for the student? What might the student be communicating?

4. When is the student less likely to engage in problem behavior? (Identify the characteristics of these situations.)

When and/or in what activities is the student most likely to engage in problem behavior? Here teams seek to uncover specific time periods, activities, or daily routines most associated with its occurrence. While it may initially seem like problem behaviors occur "all the time," careful observation often reveals that students engage in problem behaviors only during certain activities or time periods. Some problem behaviors may occur during regularly scheduled activities such as art, reading, or snack. Other behaviors occur during activities that are best defined by their characteristics, like unstructured play or one-to-one instruction, or noisy activities.

Time periods can be either related or unrelated to activities. Problem behaviors may occur only in the morning, during the afternoon, or on certain days of the week. Although the occurrences of most problem behaviors are associated with particular activities or time periods, some problem behaviors appear random and may occur during any activity or time period. Regardless, as predictable patterns emerge (even random can be a predictable pattern), you and your team are ready to answer the next question.

The second assessment question asks, *What specific antecedent or setting events are most likely to trigger to problem behaviors?* Here teams analyze problematic activities or time periods to uncover discrete antecedent events that immediately trigger problem behaviors and setting events that later set the stage for problem behaviors.

Antecedent (also known as "fast") triggers occur just before a problem behavior and can consist of just about anything a student finds problematic. Antecedent triggers may be physical stimuli (e.g., crowded room, noise level, the scent of perfume), physiological conditions (e.g., fatigue, difficulty in breathing due to a head cold or allergies), social interactions (e.g., being told what to do, reprimands, peer teasing), or activity-related events (e.g., difficult work task, disorganized materials, lost object). Also look for potential triggers in the absence of events in any one of these categories. For example, the lack of peer or social interaction, the absence of an activity (doing nothing), or the lack of a physically stimulating environment can be a trigger for problem behaviors as well. For more examples of common antecedent triggers to problem behaviors, see Table 10 in chapter 3.

Often described as "slow triggers," setting events refer to physical stimuli, physiological conditions of the student, and other social events *that occur prior to and distant from the problem behavior.* Even though setting events may be less observable than antecedents because they often occur at a distant time rather than just prior to the onset of a problem behavior, they nonetheless set the stage for problem behavior by influencing whether an antecedent event will trigger problem behavior. For example, on most days Sue responds to teacher corrections. But on days when Sue is tired (setting event), frequent teacher correction (antecedent trigger) results in Sue pounding her desk. Other examples of setting events include changes in a morning routine that make it difficult for Andrew to attend to his work in the afternoon, peer teasing on the playground that results in Patrick refusing to participate in any social activities for the remainder of the day, and a fight on the school bus that results in Amy periodically rocking back and forth throughout the school day.

Consider a third assessment question: *What function or purpose does the problem behavior serve for the student?* Or, *What could the student be communicating by engaging in the problem behavior?* Table 5 lists some common functions of problem behaviors and examples of possible communicative messages for each. You can identify function by observing what happens after a problem behavior occurs. When a problem behavior occurs, consider, *What does the student get or avoid? How do people respond?* For example, if a tantrum prolongs the start of the next activity (what the student gets), we might surmise that the student is seeking to delay or avoid that activity. If making silly animal noises during reading results in peer giggles and teacher reprimands (how people respond), we might conclude that the student is seeking some form of attention. Because the ways in which others respond to problem behaviors are not always consistent or readily observable, function may be inferred from the antecedent conditions. For example, although Mom denies Julia candy when she screams for it in the grocery store checkout line, we might infer that Julia's screaming functions to get the candy. (Actually, Grandma offers Julia candy at the slightest whine! If it works for Grandma, why not Mom?)

Finally, consider the fourth assessment question: *When is the student less likely to engage in problem behavior?* Specifically, *What are the characteristics of these situations?* Identifying when the student does not

TABLE 5

Common Functions and Communicative Intent of Problem Behavior

To gain access to social interaction	"Play with me." "Watch what I'm doing." "Did I do good work?" "Spend time with me." "Let's do this together." "Can I have a turn, too?" "I want to be one of the gang."
To gain access to activities, objects, food	"I want to play outside." "Can I have what she has?" "I want to listen to more music." "I don't want to stop; I'm enjoying this." "I'm hungry."
To terminate or avoid unwanted situations	"Leave me alone." "This is too hard. I need help." "I don't want to do this." "Don't tell me what to do." "I don't like to be teased." "I'm bored." "I'm not feeling well." "I need a break."
To gain access to sensory stimuli and to self-regulate	"I like doing this." "This calms me down." "This feels good."

engage in problem behavior can provide important contrast clues for discovering specific events that trigger problem behavior in other situations. For example, if a student does not engage in problem behavior during preferred activities, it may suggest that disliked or difficult activities are problematic for the student. Or, if a student never engages in problem behaviors when the teacher structures peer interactions during play, we might surmise that problem behaviors serve a social interaction function for the student. Moreover, asking this question may help teams to discover "what works" for the individual. Such information may be used to build positive events into the person's daily routines and prevent problem incidents.

Functional assessment tools and sources. Teams can select from any number of functional assessment tools and sources to gather the broad and specific information needed for the assessment process. See Table 6 for a description of these tools and sources. (Appendix E lists a number of books and Web sites where published functional assessment tools and examples of teacher-generated tools can be found.)

All functional assessment tools can be classified into two general methods. *Indirect methods* do not involve direct observation of the student, but rather use secondary sources such as interviews or student records for information. *Direct methods* involve direct observation of the student and data recording of observed problem behavior (including time and activity), antecedent or setting events, consequences of behavior, and perceived function.

To gather broad information, use indirect functional assessment methods such as team discussions and interviews with the student, family members, teacher assistants, and others who have had the opportunity to interact with the student across various activities and settings. Teams are encouraged to use published interview forms and rating scales to guide their discussions, as well as to generate their own self-guided questions. Review of the student's records is also useful at this step of assessment to provide information on the student's achievements, skills, medical history, and history related to problem behaviors.

Person-center planning and wraparound activities provide another avenue for gathering broad information about the student. These planning activities involve school professionals, family members, and representatives from relevant community support agencies for the purpose of coordinating supports across home, school, and community settings. When team members come together, information on any number of the broad assessment areas can be shared. For example, parents can share medical information and their perspective on the student's interests,

T A B L E   6

Sample Functional Assessment Tools

Assessment information	Method	Tool(s) or source	Use
Broad information	Indirect	Structured interviews with student, family, teachers, and other professionals *Tool:* ■ Functional Assessment Interview (O'Neill et al., 1997)	■ Gathers broad information about student health, learning style and history, school and home settings, relationships, preferences, and interests ■ Defines and prioritizes behaviors ■ Provides clues for where and when problem behaviors are most likely to occur
	Indirect	Review of school records, student IEP, progress reports, behavior support plans, and documents *Tool:* ■ Team generated	■ Provides historical information on the student's learning and on successful and unsuccessful interventions ■ Provides information on environmental, health, learning, and psychological factors related to problem behaviors
	Indirect	Person-centered planning, wraparound process *Tool:* ■ Team generated, but many resources available to guide team inquiry (e.g., Holburn, Gordon, & Vietze, 2006)	■ Gathers multiple perspectives on the student from school personnel, the family, and other service providers ■ Assesses the student's overall quality of life
Specific information	Indirect	Structured interviews with family, student, and other professionals; focuses on events surrounding problem behavior *Tools:*	■ Identifies where problem behaviors are likely to occur, potential triggers, and function of problem behavior ■ Provides information to help focus direct observations

	■ Functional Behavioral Assessment-Behavior Support Plan Protocol (Crone & Horner, 2003) ■ Student-Directed Functional Assessment Interview (e.g., O'Neill et al., 1997)	on specific settings, times of day, and triggers
Indirect	Guided team-based discussions *Tool:* ■ Initial Line of Inquiry (Knoster & Llewellyn, 2007)	■ Identifies potential triggers and function of behavior ■ Helps team form a consensus on possible hypotheses ■ Provides information to help focus direct observations on specific settings, times of day, and triggers
Direct	Direct observation of student *Tools:* ■ ABC Chart (for examples, explore Web resources) ■ Scatter Plot (Touchette, MacDonald, & Langer, 1985; see also Web resources) ■ Functional Observation Form (O'Neill et al., 1997)	■ Documents frequency of problem behaviors and activities/times in which they occur ■ Documents triggers, consequences, and perceived function of problem behaviors ■ Checklists provide suggested triggers and functions; useful when teams don't know what triggers or consequences to look for
Direct	Hypothesis tests *Tool:* ■ Team generated, but resources available to guide team (e.g., O'Neill et al., 1997)	■ Verifies triggers to problem behaviors by presenting a trigger and then removing a trigger (usually across days) and observing the effect on the presence or absence of problem behavior (e.g., alternating between easy and difficult tasks in a reading activity)

preferences, and goals. School professionals can share information on the student's current level of academic functioning in academic areas as well as information on the student's social relationships with classmates.

To gather specific information, use direct methods to observe the student during both problematic and nonproblematic situations. Some examples of direct functional assessment tools are the scatter plot, useful for identifying activities and time periods that are most problematic (or less problematic) for the student, and the ABC (antecedent-behavior-consequence) analyses in which the teacher or another team member records what is observed before (e.g., setting and antecedent events) and after (e.g., consequences, perceived function) each incident of problem behavior. Direct observation rating scales and checklists are useful when team members are unsure of what to look for when observing a student. They provide a menu of antecedent and consequence options that can be checked off as the problem behavior occurs.

Indirect methods are also useful for gathering specific information, but they should be backed up with direct observation in a comprehensive functional assessment. To illustrate, the Initial Line of Inquiry (see Appendix E, Knoster & Llewellyn, 2007) is a team-based approach for gathering specific information. Using wall charts to record and display team responses, team members use their prior observations to answer questions similar to those shown in Table 4. Indirect methods such as this one can get team members to very quickly form a consensus on possible triggers and functions of problem behaviors, but these observations should be verified by observing the student directly.

Finally, hypothesis testing is another direct method of gathering specific information. Teams use hypothesis testing when they want to verify preliminary hypotheses about specific antecedents or consequences associated with problem behavior. Because it involves introducing and then taking away events that evoke problem behavior, this method should be used judiciously, and never when the problem behavior threatens the safety of the student or others. To illustrate, Mrs. McCabe suspects that Jonathan shouts out, "I'm not doing this," when she hands him a math assignment because he easily gets overwhelmed by the number of math problems on a worksheet. So, on one day she hands him a typical worksheet and records his refusal and the number of problems solved. And then on the next day she gives him five problems at a time, up to 20, and says, "When you've finished five, and think you can handle more, let me know and I'll give you more." She repeats this process alternating between the sets of worksheets across a few days and records her observations. She verified that her hypothesis was correct because Jonathan always completed 20 problems on the days she gave him five problems at a time, but completed zero problems when she gave him the typical worksheet.

In summary, a number of functional assessment tools and sources are available to gather broad and specific information about the student and the student's problem behavior. All tools have strengths and weaknesses, and some are more time-consuming than others. The best tools are the ones that are carefully matched to your purpose and the information you wish to gather.

Generate Hypothesis Statements

Once the assessment process is completed and predictable patterns emerge that explain when and why the student engages in problem behavior, you and your team are ready to develop hypothesis statements. As described, hypothesis statements not only summarize assessment results by offering a logical explanation for problem behavior, but also guide the development of positive behavior support (PBS) plans. Interventions developed without assessment-based hypotheses are likely to be unsuccessful because they ignore the conditions contributing to the problem behavior. More important, they ignore the reason for the problem behavior from the student's perspective. Imagine being redirected back to the task when you are attempting to communicate how difficult, unpleasant, or tiring the work is. Imagine being reinforced for being "quiet" when you are trying to communicate that something is troubling you. Imagine the frustration a student might feel when a behavior-change program ignores what the student is attempting to communicate.

We recommend formulating two types of hypotheses to guide your intervention efforts: a specific hypothesis and a global hypothesis.

Specific Hypothesis

A specific hypothesis pulls together the specific information gathered during the functional assessment process. Specific hypotheses explain why a problem behavior occurs by (a) describing antecedent and setting events regularly associated with it and (b) identifying its possible function. Specific hypotheses consist of three component statements:

- **When this happens:** (a description of specific setting and antecedent events associated with the problem behavior),

- **The student does this:** (a description of the problem behavior),

- **In order to:** (a description of the possible function of the problem behavior).

Figure 3 illustrates a specific hypothesis for Elena. This hypothesis explains that Elena is most likely to engage in self-injury involving screaming, face slapping, and head banging when she is unengaged for 5 minutes or more, or when she comes to school with a cold. These episodes most likely occur during relatively unstructured school activities such as snack, lunch, and free time, but could occur at any time when Elena is unoccupied with an activity or when she is not feeling well. The possible function of Elena's self-injury is to gain teacher interaction, because observations indicate that Elena quickly quiets after the teacher calms her with touches and hugs, a soft voice, and redirection to another activity.

A specific hypothesis, such as Elena's, will drive the short-term prevention components of a behavior support plan that consists of antecedent and setting-event modifications. It provides precise information on what antecedent or setting events could be modified to prevent problem behaviors from occurring. And by identifying the possible function of the problem behavior, a specific hypothesis also provides essential information needed to teach alternative skills.

FIGURE 3

Specific Hypothesis for Elena

When this happens:

Elena is unengaged with others or materials for 5 minutes or more (particularly during snack, lunch, and free time), or she comes to school with a cold.

Elena does this:

screams, slaps her face, and bangs her head.

In order to:

gain access to teacher interaction.

Because problem behaviors serve different functions depending on the situation (e.g., head banging is used to gain teacher attention when alone and to escape difficult tasks when working), be prepared to write several specific hypotheses. Your support plan will need to address each hypothesis. Following are other illustrations of specific hypothesis statements.

- When Julia wants something and is told no, she is likely to scream and cry in an effort to get what she wants.

- When Olivia is tired and she is corrected more than twice during an activity, she will pound her desk with her fists to terminate the activity.

- If Andrew has a negative interaction on the school bus (fight, peer teasing, reprimand from the aide), he periodically rocks throughout the remainder of the school day to calm himself (obtain sensory stimulation).

- If during art or cooking Amy gets her hands messy, she'll push or throw the materials in order to stop the activity.

Global Hypothesis

Specific hypotheses are essential for building meaningful and effective support plans, but they alone cannot provide a comprehensive understanding of the complexity of conditions that might be influencing behaviors. So we highly recommend that you formulate a global hypothesis summarizing the relevant, broad information gathered during the functional assessment process. A global hypothesis addresses broad influences related to an individual's skills, health, preferences, daily routines, and overall quality of life. In effect, a global hypothesis provides a contextual explanation for why the events identified in the specific hypothesis are problematic for the person. A global hypothesis for Elena is illustrated in Figure 4.

The global hypothesis for Elena explains why being alone or having a cold is a problem, and why self-injury is used to gain teacher interaction. It suggests that Elena enjoys interacting with others and engaging in activities, but with a limited repertoire of social communication skills Elena has no way of initiating activities, communicating what she wants, or expressing that she is not feeling well. In addition to skill deficits, the global hypothesis suggests that her current classroom situation may be contributing to the problem. Placed in a classroom with other students who have significant support needs, Elena frequently finds herself waiting for teacher time while the teacher attends to others. With limited opportunities for peer interaction, Elena is totally dependent on the teacher or another adult to stay engaged. Given her current situation, Elena's self-injury is an effective way for her to bring about desired change. Her self-injury may be communicating that she wants to interact with the teacher (or other students), wants something to do, or needs comfort when she is sick.

F I G U R E 4

Global Hypothesis for Elena

Elena enjoys interacting with others and keeping busy. She seems happiest when she is interacting one-on-one with a teacher or participating in an adult-led activity in which she receives personal attention. She will occasionally sit alone for about 15 minutes when listening to a tape, although she seems to be growing bored with this activity.

Elena has no formal means of communication. Although she enjoys interacting with others, she has never been observed to initiate (other than with problem behaviors) a social interaction with her teachers or peers. Her independent play skills are severely limited to a few activities. Elena's classroom peers, who also have significant learning needs, provide little opportunity for sustained peer interaction or play. Elena has limited access to nondisabled peers at lunch and recess.

Elena's self-injury seems to signal her desire for social interaction, something to do, teacher assistance, or comfort when she is ill. Given her current situation, Elena's self-injury may be her only means of achieving these outcomes.

Global hypotheses primarily drive the long-term support component of a positive behavior support plan. They keep teams focused on expanding the individual's skills, facilitating meaningful outcomes, and improving the person's quality of life.

Summary

In this chapter we emphasized the importance of observing and assessing the student before designing a positive behavior support plan. We reviewed the basic steps and methods of conducting a functional assessment. Once you formulate specific and global hypotheses, you are ready to design a comprehensive behavior support plan as described in the next chapter. See Table 7 for a self-check summary of the steps to complete.

T A B L E   7

Self-Check for Conducting a
Comprehensive Functional Assessment

Was a functional assessment conducted before implementing a behavior support plan?	Y	N
Were both broad and specific information gathered in an effort to obtain a comprehensive understanding of the possible reasons for the problem behavior?	Y	N
Did the broad assessment contain information on the student's skills and abilities, preferences, general health, history, and overall quality of life?	Y	N
Did the specific assessment guide you in identifying (a) when the problem behavior is most and least likely to occur, (b) specific events that trigger or set the stage for the problem behavior, and (c) the function of the problem behavior?	Y	N
Were the assessment results summarized in both global and specific hypothesis statements?	Y	N
Did the specific hypotheses include the following three components: (a) when this happens (b) the individual does this (c) in order to?	Y	N
Is your team prepared to link intervention and support strategies back to the hypotheses?	Y	N

CHAPTER 3

Designing Comprehensive Positive Behavior Support Plans

Effective positive behavior support (PBS) plans are assessment based. They are linked to the specific and global hypotheses that explain problem behaviors. Once environmental influences of problem behaviors are understood, you and your team will consider *what triggers and other environmental influences can you change* so that problem behaviors can be prevented and *what can you teach* so that the student will have more socially appropriate ways of achieving desired outcomes.

Comprehensive positive behavior support plans involve multiple components that often consist of multiple interventions or support strategies. Because the goal of a PBS plan is not just to reduce problem behaviors but rather to make long-lasting, quality-of-life improvements for the student in multiple settings, it is highly unlikely that a single intervention in isolation will be effective. Moreover, because many problem behaviors are influenced by multiple environmental triggers and serve different functions in different situations or settings, teams should be prepared to develop interventions to address each unique situation.

To be maximally effective, PBS plans must also fit the student's environmental and social contexts. That is, in order for student gains to be maintained over time, they should be designed to reflect student (and family) priorities, preferences, interests, and goals. Furthermore, support plans should be designed to fit the settings in which they will be implemented to ensure that the interventions can be carried out and maintained. All settings differ with respect to daily routines and demands. Settings also differ with respect to the capacity and preferences of the people responsible for implementing a behavior support plan.

Thus, what may be doable in one setting (e.g., in one classroom or at home) may not be doable in another setting because of these differences. Teams should be prepared to tailor selected interventions to the particular characteristics of each setting as well as to the skills and preferences of the plan implementers.

Designing a "good" comprehensive support plan, one that can be realistically carried out and result in desired change, will require you and your team to collaborate, problem solve, and select the best interventions in order to address several dimensions of effectiveness. In the final analysis, you will discover that no two support plans will be entirely alike. Each will be individually tailored to the student's unique needs, skills and preferences, and settings. Table 8 presents considerations for designing good comprehensive PBS plans.

T A B L E   8
Designing "Good" (Effective) Comprehensive PBS Plans

- Does the support plan address the student's needs as identified in the specific and global hypotheses?

- Is the support plan comprehensive? Does it
  - involve multiple support plan components?
  - address multiple triggers or functions?
  - address multiple settings?

- Does the support plan reflect student preferences, interests, and goals?

- Does the support plan reflect parent priorities and preferences?

- Is the support plan doable? Is it
  - matched to daily routines or setting characteristics?
  - matched to the abilities of the implementers?

Chapter Purpose

Comprehensive PBS plans typically consist of four key components: (1) antecedent and setting-event modifications, also known as short-term prevention strategies, (2) teaching alternative skills, (3) consequence

interventions, and (4) long-term supports. In this chapter we describe the process for selecting or designing interventions for each component and explain how the various components work in concert with one another to contribute to the long-term effectiveness of a support plan.

For each component we discuss specific advantages and limitations, give examples of strategies, and offer guiding questions that may be useful in your team's selection of strategies. (See Appendix A for a complete list of guiding questions.) To illustrate how each of the components is used, we continue the example of Elena throughout the chapter. (See Appendix B for a summary of Elena's support plan.)

In practice, you and your team will most likely consider the four intervention components simultaneously because each component to various degrees is dependent on other components for the overall success of a behavior support plan and is not intended to be used alone. However, for clarity, we present the components linearly beginning with the quick-acting antecedent and setting-event modifications and moving toward the long-term support strategies. There are circumstances under which your team may want to prioritize the order in which components are implemented. (For this discussion see chapter 5.)

• •

Clarke and colleagues demonstrated the effectiveness of a comprehensive, multicomponent support plan for a 12-year-old student with intense problem behaviors. Multiple positive outcomes were observed including (a) reduction in problem behaviors across settings, (b) higher ratings of student happiness, (c) improved social interactions with others, and (d) perceived increases in the student's overall quality of life.

—Clarke, Worchester, Dunlap, Murray, & Bradley-Klug, 2002

Antecedent and Setting-Event Modifications

Advantages

Effective teachers know that the most successful classroom management strategies are proactive and preventive in nature. By acting before problem behaviors occur (such as stating clear expectations for desired behaviors or modifying seating arrangements), teachers can prevent most problem situations from arising. Antecedent and setting-event modifications (or just antecedent modifications for short) are proactive. Unlike general-classroom management strategies, antecedent interventions address student-specific triggers that immediately set off or later set the stage for problem behavior. Once your team identifies specific events that seem to trigger problem behavior, you can change these events by eliminating or modifying them and thereby prevent problem behavior from occurring.

There are at least two primary benefits of using antecedent modifications. First, they are powerful and quick acting because they change or take away the events that trigger problem behaviors. Therefore, antecedent and setting-event modifications can immediately reduce problem behavior through prevention. From the individual's perspective, antecedent modifications provide immediate relief from frustrating or problematic situations. From a teacher's perspective, antecedent modifications provide the opportunity to teach alternative skills and build supportive environments, instead of reacting to the student in crisis. Second, antecedent modifications avoid the problems and negative consequences often associated with reactive interventions. By preventing problem behavior, students may avoid the risk of being excluded from activities as teachers and students maintain positive interactions. Antecedent and setting-event modifications are considered short-term prevention strategies because they are often temporary solutions for preventing problem behaviors. Antecedent and setting-event modifications can be faded or removed from a student's support plan once the student learns alternative skills or more permanent adaptations or once long-term supports are put into place.

• •

Problem behavior can be avoided by modifying known antecedent and setting events. Modifications can be readily incorporated into curricular and daily school routines.

—Kern, Choutka, & Sokol, 2002

Strategies

When selecting or designing antecedent modifications, consider two important questions: (1) *How can the triggering antecedent or setting event be changed so that problem behaviors can be prevented?* Specifically, consider how the problematic events identified in the student's specific hypothesis can be modified in home, school, or community settings to avoid problem behavior. (2) *What can be added to the student's daily routines to make desired behaviors more likely and situations more pleasant for the student?* As a team, reflect on the functional assessment information and clues in the hypothesis statements to identify specific activities, events, or interactions that may result in success for the student.

Table 9 summarizes five major types of antecedent modifications you can make once the triggering antecedent and/or setting event has been identified. For example, you can *remove* or eliminate a triggering event to avoid a problem behavior. If eliminating an event entirely is not possible or desirable, you can change or *modify* the trigger in some way (i.e., make it better) so that it no longer creates a problem for the individual. When unpleasant or difficult tasks must be done (such as personal hygiene, some academic tasks) and are difficult to modify, you can *intersperse* them among easier or more pleasant tasks. Such an approach makes unpleasant events more tolerable, reducing the likelihood that the student will seek to avoid them through problem behaviors. You may also *add events* to the person's daily routines that encourage positive behaviors. Students are less likely to engage in problem behaviors when engaged in activities they enjoy. Finally, for setting events that you cannot prevent from occurring (e.g., coming down with a cold), you may *block* or neutralize their influence on student behaviors by intervening with another activity. For example, if a student is not feeling well, you

Antecedent and Setting-Event Modifications

Strategies	Instructional examples	Social or health examples
Remove a problem event.	■ Avoid giving difficult word problems for independent seatwork ■ Avoid requiring repetitive tasks (e.g., writing out spelling words)	■ Avoid giving caffeinated drinks ■ Avoid bringing student to large crowds ■ Avoid exposing student to long delays
Modify a problem event.	■ Shorten lessons ■ Reduce the number of problems on a page ■ Modify instruction to decrease errors (e.g., errorless learning strategy) ■ Increase lesson pace	■ Change voice intonation ■ Modify a boring schedule ■ Use suggestive rather than directive language (e.g., "What should you do now?") ■ Increase fiber in diet ■ Treat the illness
Intersperse difficult or unpleasant events with easy or pleasant events	■ Mix difficult word problems with easy ones ■ Mix mastered tasks with acquisition tasks for independent seatwork	■ Schedule nonpreferred activities (e.g., cleaning) among preferred activities (e.g., leisure) ■ Precede directives for nonpreferred activities (e.g., "Brush your teeth") with easily followed directives (e.g., "Open the cabinet; choose your favorite toothpaste")
Add events that promote desired behaviors	■ Provide choice of tasks, materials, and activities ■ Include student preferences in curriculum development (e.g., meaningful, functional curriculum) ■ Use cooperative learning strategies to encourage participation ■ State clear expectations for student performance at the start of each lesson	■ Schedule preferred activities in daily routines; involve student in planning to increase predictability ■ Provide a rich variety of activities from which to choose ■ Provide increased opportunities for social interactions before problems arise ■ Provide opportunities for daily exercise ■ Promote a healthy diet

Strategies	Instructional examples	Social or health examples
Block or neutralize the impact of negative events	■ Allow the individual to take frequent breaks during difficult work activities ■ Reduce academic demands when the student appears agitated or upset	■ Provide opportunities for rest when the student is tired or ill ■ Provide time alone or time to regroup after a negative experience

can reduce the number of difficult demands that day to avoid problem behaviors. Table 9 provides examples of each of the five types of antecedent modifications with specific examples applied to instructional, social, and health situations.

The number of possible antecedent and setting-event modifications is almost limitless. Potential modifications are as varied as the number of triggers that set off problem behaviors. Each modification must be carefully selected to match the student's needs and the situation or setting in which they will be applied. Table 10 presents some other examples and an alternative way of classifying antecedent and setting-event modifications. In this table we list common antecedent triggers grouped by the four main functions of problem behavior. We then give examples of antecedent and setting-event modifications that are supported by research.

• •

Elena

Elena's teacher and team considered the two guiding questions posed earlier. As identified in her specific hypothesis, Elena was more likely to engage in self-injury when she was unengaged for 5 minutes or more during unstructured school activities such as snack, free play, or lunch. During these situations Elena often spent time alone or unoccupied as the teacher or assistant attended to the other students. Elena was less likely to engage in challenging behaviors during structured, teacher-led activities where teacher interaction was frequent and activity participation was high.

T A B L E   1 0
Antecedent Modifications:
Common Triggers and Intervention Examples

Function	Common triggers	Intervention examples
To gain access to social interaction or attention	■ Unengaged for periods of time ■ Sees another getting attention or interacting socially ■ Wants to initiate an interaction ■ Few opportunities for social interaction ■ Has to wait for social opportunities	■ Provide attention *before* problem behavior occurs · Teacher schedules a "special time" to chat when the student arrives at school · Teacher directs peers to comment on the student's good work ■ Build opportunities for meaningful social interaction into the school day · Use cooperative learning groups · Make use of peer buddies into the school day · Have student serve as teacher helper ■ Provide enjoyable alternative activities when the student has to wait · Favorite book or magazine · Computer game ■ Provide cues for initiating positive social interactions · Picture brag book to share with peers · Cue cards on how and what to say to start conversations with peers
To gain access (or maintain) an activity or object	■ Seeing something wanted ■ Being told "no" or "not now" ■ Transition to another activity ■ Restricted access to desired activities/materials	■ Use scheduling to enhance predictability · Show when a preferred activity will occur · If "no," show when it will happen ■ Provide alternative options · "You can't have ice cream now, but you can have some juice or cookies." ■ Ease transitions · Provide warning that the activity will terminate · Announce and embed a preferred activity in the next transition activity (e.g., start next activity with a brief game) ■ Make restricted materials more accessible · Fill one cabinet with healthy food snacks

Function	Common triggers	Intervention examples
To terminate or avoid something disliked or unwanted	■ Few opportunities to control or self-direct activities ■ Activity is difficult ■ Activity is disliked, not relevant, or personally meaningful ■ Social interaction is negative	■ Provide opportunities for choice and self-direction · Have the student select and self-manage learning goals · Have the student schedule the sequence of learning activities · Provide choice options between activities and within activities to make disliked activities more enjoyable (e.g., choices of materials, people to work with, ways to accomplish objectives) ■ Adjust the difficulty of the work task · Embed difficult activities among easy ones; increase the proportion of easy vs. difficult · Pre-teach · Provide difficult work in small chunks · Provide opportunities for taking a break; shorten the activity ■ Increase the meaningfulness of tasks · Modify/select activities relevant to student interests or goals · Modify the mode of completed work (e.g., computer vs. pencil) ■ Modify the style of interaction · Change the style, pace of instruction · Use errorless prompting strategies to avoid errors · Structure activities for positive peer comments
To gain access to sensory stimuli	■ Over- or under-stimulating environment ■ Unpleasant or noxious sensory stimuli	■ Modify/enrich the environment · Fill setting with interesting activities · Provide alternatives to sensory stimulation (e.g., visual toy for student seeking visual stimulation) ■ Avoid or shield student from events the student finds unpleasant or upsetting · Avoid crowded activities · Offer earplugs during fire drills

The antecedent modifications in Elena's support plan were based on an initial goal of making the unstructured activities more like the teacher-led activities. Specifically, the team decided to structure snack, free time, and lunch so that Elena would have more opportunities for teacher (and peer) interaction and participation in activities. The team reasoned that providing these opportunities would create a situation in which Elena would have little reason to engage in problem behaviors.

By observing what was "working" for Elena during teacher-led activities, Mrs. Gallago and the teacher assistant believed they could modify the unstructured activities in the following ways: First, they could stay close to Elena. This would allow more opportunities for casual conversation and teacher turn-taking. For example, during outside play, Mrs. Gallago could alternate between pushing Elena and another child on the swings. Second, the staff could involve Elena in teacher activities, such as passing out cookies for snack or assisting with the other students. Elena also might try pushing Roberto on the swings. Third, if teacher interaction was not possible, the teachers agreed to adjust their schedules so that Elena would never be unattended for more than 5 minutes at a time. Before leaving her, they would try offering Elena an independent activity such as listening to music; they recognized that this option was limited, given that Elena could become bored. Still, if not overly used, the teachers believed this modification was worth trying.

When Elena came to school with a cold, she was likely to engage in self-injury during most any school activity. Although it seemed Elena was seeking adult interaction, the teachers could not be sure about what Elena was communicating. Was she seeking comfort or reassurance? Was she asking the teacher for a rest? Was she asking for a change of activities, perhaps less demanding ones? On days when Elena was not feeling well, the teachers decided to check on Elena frequently during all school activities, particularly attending to her nonverbal cues that might signal discomfort. They would offer her frequent choices to terminate, change activities, or rest.

Considerations

In summary, by changing the conditions that are problematic for the individual, antecedent and setting-event modifications can prevent problem behaviors from occurring, bringing about immediate relief for the student and teacher. But this component is limited in that it may not be effective in the long run. The success of antecedent and setting-event modifications often depends on a carefully arranged environment. In the event that the teacher cannot prevent problem situations, or the student goes to another setting in which modifications are not in place, challenging behaviors are likely to recur. Longer lasting results are achieved by helping students learn the skills needed to control their own environments (alternative skill training) and by creating long-term supports to maintain and generalize new skills and enhance their quality of life.

Antecedent modifications are considered short-term prevention strate-gies because they can be eliminated once the student learns new skills or the team implements long-term supports. But some short-term modifications may become permanent accommodations that should be kept in place long term to help the student successfully participate in daily activities. For instance, for many individuals with developmental disabilities, picture schedules are vital tools for helping them to plan and predict what will happen in the future. Because picture schedules can improve individuals' functional capacity, they are an example of an antecedent modification that should not be eliminated, but rather used permanently for participation in daily activities.

Some may ask, Why use antecedent modifications at all? After all, by modifying the environment, the student is denied the opportunity to learn how to deal with difficult situations. For example, when difficult math problems are adapted or removed in order to avoid tantrums, the student does not learn how to deal with frustration or, more important, does not learn how to do the task. In Elena's case, the concern might be that antecedent modifications are preventing her from learning how to cope with being alone.

As we see it, when antecedent and setting-event modifications are used in conjunction with other support components (e.g., alternative skill training, long-term supports), they create positive, respectful conditions that are conducive to learning. It is extremely difficult both to teach and to learn when the student is engaging in frequent problem behaviors because of unchanged conditions. Learning occurs best in situations that are pleasant, respectful, and responsive to personal needs.

Teaching Alternative Skills

Advantages

Positive behavior support should teach students alternative means for achieving their desired outcomes. Typically, students with disabilities engage in challenging behaviors because (a) they do not have the skills (or are not fluent in the skills) to meet their needs or (b) they have learned that these behaviors can bring about desired results (e.g., whining to get something is often more effective than appropriately asking). Whichever the case, your aim is not to ignore the students' goals, but to help them achieve desired outcomes through acceptable alternatives that are both effective and efficient. Teaching alternative skills contributes to long-term reduction of problem behavior, because students are able to achieve desired outcomes and prevent problem situations from occurring, as well as cope effectively with difficult situations. Students are less dependent on teacher modifications once alternative skills are learned.

• •

Functional communication training has resulted in students using functional alternatives to problem behaviors years after instruction. Further, students who were instructed in the classroom, were able to use their functional alternatives in community settings with adults who were not involved in training.

—Durand, 1999; Durand & Carr, 1991

Strategies

Alternative skill instruction can be categorized into three distinct approaches: (1) teaching replacement skills, (2) teaching general skills, and (3) teaching coping skills. See Table 11 for definitions and examples of each approach.

TABLE 11
Alternative Skills Interventions

Alternative skills to be taught	Examples
Replacement skills One-to-one replacement skills that serve the same function as the problem behavior	■ Teach the student to communicate (e.g., "I need help") to replace head banging to escape difficult work ■ Teach the student to initiate social interactions (e.g., "Play with me") to replace teasing peers as a form of initiation ■ Teach the student to play a video game, to replace finger flicking during "down" times
General skills Broad skills that alter problem situations and prevent the need for problem behaviors	■ Teach organizational skills to prevent the individual from becoming frustrated when faced with multiple tasks ■ Expand social play skills so that the child has more opportunities to make friends ■ Teach the individual to self-initiate activities using a picture schedule to prevent boredom
Coping skills Skills that teach students to cope with or tolerate difficult situations	■ Use desensitization techniques to teach the individual to accept medical examinations or tolerate fire drills ■ Teach the student to relax during stressful events ■ Teach the student negotiation or conflict resolution skills ■ Teach the student to control angry outbursts

Teaching Replacement Skills

Here you teach the student to use an alternative action during problematic situations that serves the same function as the problem behavior.

Referring back to the specific hypothesis, consider the guiding question, *When a problem situation arises, what alternative skill could the student use that would serve the same function as the problem behavior?* For example, if Quinn pushes his materials off the table in an effort to terminate his work even though he has not completed it, an appropriate replacement skill might be to communicate, "I'm done!" which would allow Quinn to end the activity more appropriately. Here pushing materials off the table and saying, "I'm done," achieve the same outcome. If Briana darts across the room to get the teacher to turn on a DVD, then an appropriate replacement skill might be to communicate, "Movie, please." Darting across the room and saying, "Movie, please," serve the same function. Selecting an alternative skill that serves the same function as the problem behavior is critical for success. Once the individual discovers that an alternative can be more or at least as effective in bringing about desired results, problem behaviors are less likely to occur.

Teaching replacement skills can bring about an immediate change for the student. However, this approach is limited because it does not address the underlying reasons for the problem behavior. In Quinn's case, the alternative, "I'm done," may effectively replace his pushing materials to the floor, but it does not address why Quinn wants to stop working before his work is completed. Is it because the work is too difficult? Does he tire easily? Is the work boring? Does he have the skills to complete his work successfully without frustration? Does he know how to pace himself to prevent fatigue? Does he know how to make choices of alternative tasks or negotiate different activities with his teacher? While important, one-to-one replacement skills do not, by themselves, give students the skills needed to circumvent problem situations.

Teaching General Skills
Teaching general skills, on the other hand, involves expanding competence so that students have more options for addressing problem situations and can prevent them from occurring.

A key guiding question to address is, *What general skills (e.g., social, communication, leisure, academic) might help the student prevent problem situations?* Referring back to the broad hypothesis for problem behavior, the following issues should be considered: (a) What factors seem to be contributing to the problem situation (e.g., word problems are too difficult for Quinn)? (b) Does the student have the skills to effectively address these factors (e.g., Quinn doesn't seem able to identify the math operation in the word problem)? (c) What skills can be taught to help the student successfully alter the situation (e.g., teach a word-problem-solving skill)? As shown in Table 11, general-skill training can involve a variety of skills such as problem solving, self-management, choice making, communication, social interaction, academics, and leisure/recreation. The goal is to expand competence in relevant areas so that the student has in his or her repertoire a variety of socially acceptable options for achieving desired outcomes and responding to and changing problem situations. Instructional strategies for teaching general skills are those commonly employed by teachers to teach any new skill.

Teaching Coping Skills

As it is for all of us, sometimes students are confronted with problem situations that cannot or should not be avoided, or times when needs cannot be met immediately. For instance, Jacob runs and screams when he hears a fire alarm. Although the sound clearly upsets him, learning to tolerate it is essential because fire drills are a regular part of school life and responding appropriately is important to his safety as well as the safety of others. Katie, on the other hand, does not like to lose a game, and will flop to the floor or attempt to kick her classmates when she does not win. Learning to cope with delays in reinforcement (winning) without engaging in problem behavior becomes an important life lesson because Katie will encounter the possibility of losing again and again whenever she plays a game.

At such times, when problem situations cannot or should not be avoided, the student needs to learn how to cope (or be tolerant) with difficult situations or reasonable delays. Consider this guiding question: *What skills are needed to help the student cope with potentially difficult or frustrating situations that cannot or should not be avoided?* Targets for instruction might include teaching the student how to control anger, wait patiently for an activity, relax or "take five" during stressful events, and persist through difficult activities perhaps by setting and self-monitoring incremental goals. Another instructional target might include systematic desensitization, in which the student is gradually exposed to situations she finds undesirable. One word of caution, however; coping skills are difficult to teach because we are essentially asking students to work through unpleasant events that they seek to avoid. To reduce resistance to learning, temporarily use antecedent modifications wherever possible to lessen the unpleasantness of the situation as the student acquires new skills. For example, in Katie's case, games can be arranged temporarily so that Katie loses at most only one out of eight games or so. This will make coping easier for her to learn, as opposed to being expected to cope with successive and frequent losses when games are left to chance. In addition, consider providing extra incentives or rewards for the student when he or she is coping through difficult events, and be sure to provide strong words of encouragement and praise for a job well done (e.g., "I know you don't like to lose, but you are such a good sport. Good for you!").

• •

Elena

Considering each guiding question, Elena's team identified three sets of alternative skills.

First, to provide Elena with an alternative way to access teacher attention during "alone" periods, the team targeted hand raising to replace self-injury. Given that Elena has no symbolic system of communication at this point, options were limited to nonverbal gestures. Hand raising was selected because it met multiple criteria needed for success. It served the same function as the problem behavior (soliciting teacher interaction), it was an easy response for Elena to learn, and it was a universally understood signal for seeking attention or assistance in school and other settings. Moreover, hand raising is an open-ended request that can serve a variety of communicative messages. The team reasoned that once Elena raised her hand, the teacher or another adult could respond by offering Elena a variety of options (e.g., Would you like to play in the sandbox? Would you like to help me push Roberto on the swing? Would you like to take a walk with me?) as Elena's interests were likely to vary.

The team also focused on expanding Elena's general skills. When Elena's team asked why Elena didn't like to be alone and why she frequently sought teacher interaction, they speculated that Elena had very few options for other social interaction or activity. (See Elena's global hypothesis, Figure 4.) She lacked a communication system so she could tell others what she wanted; she did not know how to occupy herself (i.e., play independently) during unstructured times; and she did not have the appropriate social skills needed to sustain peer interactions. Each of these areas became a target for instruction. As for an initial communication system, Mrs. Gallago decided to teach Elena how to use a picture communication book to make simple requests for activities. She paired Elena's use of the book with hand raising. First, Elena could raise her hand, requesting teacher attention, then Mrs. Gallago or the assistant could guide Elena to point to a desired activity. To expand independent play skills, Mrs. Gallago would expose Elena to a variety of options, then systematically teach Elena how to play with preferred toys or activities. To expand social skills, Mrs. Gallago would teach Elena how to make simple reciprocal exchanges during a play activity with a peer (e.g., offer materials, share materials, take turns). This plan would require greater opportunities for peer interaction than Elena's current classroom provided. (We discuss this more in the later section "Long-Term Support.")

The team also considered coping skills for Elena. As Elena learned new skills, being unoccupied was less likely to be a problem for her. Nevertheless, there were going to be times when Elena would need to wait for teacher assistance or to participate in an activity, as requests could not always be met immediately. To teach Elena to be patient, Mrs. Gallago decided to acknowledge Elena's hand raising (e.g., "Okay, Elena, I will be with you in a minute"), then slowly increase the time between the acknowledgment and the teacher's response (e.g., "What do you want to do?"). Teaching Elena to wait would be taught only after Elena had successfully learned to raise her hand to signal teacher attention. Teaching waiting while also teaching an alternative communication response is likely to result in Elena's continued use of the problem behavior. (See the following section, "Considerations.")

Considerations

We discussed three approaches to teaching and selecting alternative skills. Consider these further tips for successful planning and instruction.

Be sure a replacement skill serves the same function as does the problem behavior. If the replacement skill does not produce the same purpose in the same or a shorter amount of time as does the problem behavior, it will not be effective for the individual.

Select easy replacement skills. When selecting a replacement skill, choose one that is relatively easy for the student to learn. If the alternative skill takes more effort to produce than the problem behavior, the student will not consistently use it. Hand raising was selected for Elena because, in comparison with other alternatives (e.g., sign language or a verbal response), it required the least amount of effort to learn.

Teach skills that produce an immediate payoff first. Initially teach those skills that bring about the quickest results for the student. By doing so, problem behaviors will be reduced rapidly, making it easier and more enjoyable for the individual to learn more skills. In Elena's case, signaling for teacher attention was taught first because it gave Elena an immediate means of addressing her needs. Teaching Elena to wait would be taught only after Elena learned that hand raising was an effective strategy for obtaining teacher attention.

Teach before problem behaviors occur. During or immediately after a problem situation occurs is often the wrong time to teach an alternative skill. Typically, people are not receptive to learning when they are upset. And teaching following an incident may inadvertently teach the individual to first engage in the problem behavior, then use the alternative response (e.g., "First I will push my books on to the floor, then I will ask for help!").

Teaching before means providing opportunities to practice new skills before the person encounters a problem situation. Strategies may include active rehearsal in simulated or actual activities (e.g., teaching Quinn what to do when he encounters a difficult word problem) and frequent reminders to use the alternative skill at the start of an activity (e.g., "Remember, Quinn, try the problem first, but if you can't do it, call me for help"). In Elena's case, Mrs. Gallago prompted Elena to raise her hand after Elena was alone for just 1 or 2 minutes. (Problem behaviors typically occurred after 5 minutes.) Prompting Elena after 1 or 2 minutes helped Elena to identify when to raise her hand (when alone or unengaged) and also occurred sufficiently in advance to avoid problem incidents.

Whenever possible, choose alternative skills that can be used across different situations and settings. The goal here is not to teach alternative skills that are useful in just one situation, but to teach skills that have the widest applicability across multiple situations. To produce the greatest effect for the student, consider alternative skills that (a) can be used across situations, (b) are easily understood by others, and (c) are appropriate across a variety of settings.

• •

*To be effective in replacing problem behaviors, alternative skills
must be more efficient to use than the problem behavior and
be acceptable, understood, and responded to by significant others.*

—Durand & Merges, 2001

Consequence Interventions

Advantages

At one time, consequence interventions (e.g., what you do after a problem behavior occurs) were synonymous with behavior management. That is, they were typically the only attempts to change problem behaviors. Although consequence strategies continue to play an important role in positive behavior support plans, they no longer predominate, because of the powerful contributions of the other support components.

When used along with the other components, especially teaching alternative skills, consequence strategies are effective teaching tools. They are used first to reinforce the individual's use of alternative skills, and second, to reduce the effectiveness of problem behaviors should they continue to occur. So a goal of consequence interventions is to teach students that (a) alternative skills are a better strategy for bringing about desired results, and (b) problem behaviors are ineffective, inefficient, or a socially undesirable means for achieving goals.

Consequence interventions also include crisis management—reactive strategies used to safely prevent students who engage in certain problem behaviors (e.g., aggression, self-injury, property destruction) from hurting themselves and others or damaging their surroundings. Crisis management does not contribute to the teaching aspect of the plan. It is purely an emergency procedure used to protect the individual and/or others from harm and to de-escalate crisis situations should other approaches in the support plan fail to prevent dangerous behaviors from occurring.

Strategies

When planning for consequence interventions, consider how you and others will respond when the student uses alternative skills or engages in problem behavior. As in all the strategies discussed thus far, there is no one best consequence approach for increasing the use of alternative skills and decreasing the incidence of problem behaviors. The best approach is tailored to the individual's ability, comprehension, and the situations described in the hypothesis statements. Examples of consequence strategies are presented in Table 12.

Consider the following three guiding questions in your planning. *How will you (or others) reinforce the student's use of alternative skills so they become more effective and efficient than the problem behavior?* Your goal is to teach the student that desired outcomes may be achieved more effectively when alternative skills are used. We do this by reinforcing the use of alternative skills while diminishing or eliminating rewards for problem behaviors.

Consider developing a reinforcement strategy for each alternative skill you intend to teach. When teaching a replacement skill, the most powerful consequence is a consistent response that provides the same outcome or function as the problem behavior. For example, when Quinn announces, "I'm done!" the teacher quickly responds by taking his

TABLE 12
Consequence Interventions

Intervention purpose	Intervention examples
Increase use of alternative skills	*Replacement skills* ■ Respond to all appropriate requests for a "break" immediately and consistently ■ Prompt peers to respond to the child's requests for play
	General or coping and tolerance skills ■ Use praise and give stickers as rewards for solving word problems ■ Have the individual self-record instances of controlling anger
Reduce outcomes of problem behavior	■ Redirect the individual to another activity or prompt him or her to use an alternative skill ■ Provide corrective feedback (e.g., "No, don't hurt John") ■ Implement age-appropriate negative consequences (e.g., loss of privileges, time-out, restitution)
Crisis management	■ At first signs of crisis, engage the individual in a calming activity ■ Clear others from the area; make room safer ■ Block hits to prevent self-injury

materials away. When Briana appropriately asks for a movie, her mother responds by turning on the DVD player. In addition, it is important to strengthen the student's use of replacement skills by responding immediately and consistently (every time) to each request, especially when the individual is first learning the replacement skill. The alternative skill must be more powerful than the problem behavior. If during initial learning the response is delayed (e.g., "Do five more problems, Quinn") or inconsistent (e.g., the teacher sometimes honors Quinn's request to finish), the student may likely continue to use the problem behavior because it will effectively bring about desired results (e.g., pushing materials on the floor will always terminate an activity). Again, we recommend teaching students to tolerate delays after the student has learned to communicate through alternative means.

For strengthening general skills and coping skills, develop a reinforcement strategy as you would teach any social or academic skill. Whenever possible, select consequences that are natural to the targeted skill, such as praise, social interaction, or access to a preferred activity, so the student will continue to use the alternative in everyday settings. You may consider the use of less naturally occurring reinforcers, such as self-recording or self-monitoring, stickers, earned privileges, and rewards for alternative skills that are especially difficult to learn. For example, teaching a student to control his or her anger during stressful situations may initially require added incentives during the acquisition phase.

The second guiding question asks your team to consider how you will respond to the student when he or she engages in the problem behavior. *How will you teach the student that the problem behavior is no longer effective, efficient, or desirable?* You will want to help the student learn that problem behaviors will no longer produce desired outcomes; they are socially unacceptable responses.

To diminish rewards for problem behavior, consider simple "ignore" strategies in which you "respond" as if the problem behavior is not occurring. For example, as the student begins to tantrum, carry on with whatever activity you were engaging in, being careful to ignore the problem behavior and not the child.

When problem behaviors cannot or should not be ignored, consider redirecting to another activity or prompting the individual to use an alternative skill. To teach the student that problem behaviors are not appropriate, consider giving corrective feedback that provides clear behavioral expectations and limits. Only verbal feedback may be needed, but sometimes additional age-appropriate interventions are warranted, as it is important to expose students to "natural consequences" established by the rules of school, family, or society, such as paying for a broken window at school or losing TV privileges at home. Be sure that consequences are consistent and no more intrusive than those used with peers who do not have disabilities.

The third question refers to crisis management and should be considered when there is a possibility that the student will engage in very serious challenging behaviors. *What can be done to de-escalate crisis situations and protect the student and others from harm?* When developing crisis intervention plans, teams should (a) carefully define what constitutes a "crisis situation," (b) describe the intervention procedures and who will be involved, and (c) identify the resources needed to both implement and document the use of the crisis plan, such as modifying the classroom schedule or calling another teacher for assistance.

Crisis management plans should be developed around the three phases of a crisis. During the escalation phase, consider how a crisis may be avoided. Does the student provide a behavioral signal that a crisis is about to erupt (e.g., increased agitation, high-pitched verbalizations)? At the onset of the first signal, what can be done to calm the student or change a potentially threatening situation (e.g., direct the student to a calming activity, "talk the student down," change the activity level in the room)? The goal of this stage is to defuse or de-escalate the impending crisis as quickly as possible. This is not a teachable moment.

At the eruption stage, consider emergency procedures that will protect the individual and others from harm. Consider protective actions, such as placing a pillow under a child's head to block the blows of self-injury, removing other people from the area, escorting the student to another location away from others, or removing objects that could be used to injure others. Choose the safest, least intrusive means possible. If physical intervention is necessary, such as restraint, use the minimum amount of contact necessary to stop or interrupt the harmful act; but be careful. Physical intervention can cause some students to increase their aggression and result in staff misapplying physical force to control the situation. Such situations can lead to serious student and staff injury, and even student death through suffocation as documented in some cases. Never use strategies that can cause more harm than good.

At the de-escalation stage, consider strategies that will keep the student calm and reintroduce her back to the day's typical activities. Try to stay close to and reassure the student at this time. Also, after a crisis event, consider what factors led up to the situation, so that crises can be prevented in the future.

Remember, crisis management interventions are used for emergencies only and should not be relied on for the long-term reduction of problem behaviors. Continued or frequent use of crisis management should signal that the other components of the support plan are not working and should be reevaluated and modified.

• •

Elena

Elena's team considered the three guiding questions while developing consequence strategies for teaching alternative skills and decreasing Elena's use of problem behavior. To replace screaming and self-injury, the team helped Elena learn that hand raising was a more effective strategy for gaining the teacher's attention. To do so, Mrs. Gallago and the teacher assistant agreed to respond immediately and consistently every time Elena raised her hand, whether the action was prompted by an adult or initiated by Elena. Initially, Mrs. Gallago was concerned that responding to each of Elena's requests would be disruptive to other students in the classroom, if not impossible to consistently implement. But she concluded that responding to Elena's outbursts was more disruptive and using antecedent modifications would actually lessen Elena's need to request teacher attention; the strategies would keep Elena actively engaged during typical school routines.

Strategies for strengthening Elena's use of general alternative skills included teacher praise and natural consequences inherent in each of the skills, such as honoring Elena's requests made by picture communication, playing with a preferred toy (independent play), and interacting with a friend (social play). Mrs. Gallago built social play and communicative opportunities around Elena's preferences to ensure that the "consequences" were indeed reinforcing. The team proposed that when it was time to teach Elena to wait for teacher assistance, praise and bright colorful stickers placed in a collector's book would provide an incentive for learning. (Waiting itself is not likely to be reinforcing.) The team reasoned that as Elena learned to occupy herself and came to trust that others would respond to her requests, waiting would be less of a problem for her.

Elena's team was confident that teaching alternative skills and using antecedent modifications would help Elena reduce her problem behavior. Nevertheless, they developed a contingency plan for when problem behaviors did occur. If Elena screamed or slapped her face, the teacher or assistant would direct Elena to raise her hand or to use her communication book so that Elena would learn that the alternative skills, not the problem behaviors, would bring about desired results. The team considered "ignoring" or not responding until Elena stopped screaming before prompting her, but this was obviously unsafe. Left unattended, screaming would erupt into face slapping and dangerous head banging.

Redirecting Elena to use alternative skills at the first sign of problem behavior also served as the first step in the crisis management plan. Redirection frequently prevented a crisis. In the event that the teachers missed Elena's early signals and she began to hurt herself, one of the teachers would respond by gently holding Elena's hands down, and, if necessary, holding Elena's upper body and arms to prevent head banging. Once Elena was calm, the teacher would stay close to Elena until she rejoined the classroom activity. Crisis management required team effort among Mrs. Gallago, the teacher assistant, and other school staff. As one teacher attended to Elena, the other managed the class, modified scheduled activities, and sought additional assistance if necessary.

Considerations

In summary, consequence strategies are useful teaching tools in a positive behavior support plan. They reinforce the student's use of alternative skills, while decreasing the effectiveness of problem behaviors. Consequence strategies are also used in emergency situations to protect the individual and others from harm. Listed below are other important considerations for successful planning.

Be sure consequence strategies are implemented along with other intervention components. It may be tempting to use consequence strategies alone, because they can be effective in the short term. But note that they cannot bring about long-term results without also teaching alternative skills or changing conditions that trigger problem behavior. In fact, using them in isolation might lead to increasingly intrusive interventions as previous attempts fail.

Understand how consequence strategies address your hypotheses. Know how each selected strategy will encourage the student's use of alternative skills and discourage problem behavior according to (a) the contributing factors identified in the student's hypotheses and (b) the student's level of comprehension. For example, it doesn't make sense to use in-class time-out (even if it is a standard classroom procedure) when Quinn pushes his materials off his desk, because such an approach would only teach Quinn that pushing materials is an effective way to end an activity. A more effective approach would be to teach Quinn an alternative way to stop his work, while simultaneously modifying his seatwork and gradually increasing demands for work completion. It is equally inappropriate to enforce a consequence that is beyond a student's comprehension, such as requiring a student to pay for a broken mirror when the student does not understand the value of money.

Be sure there is a clear understanding of what crisis management is, what constitutes an emergency, and how to respond. Crisis management uses the least intrusive means to prevent students from hurting themselves or others and damaging their surroundings. To prevent injury or damage, consider the least intrusive intervention first. Can furniture be moved? Can others be asked to leave the setting? Can self-injury be blocked or interrupted by moving the individual away from the wall or other hard surfaces? If physical restraint is the only safety option, then extreme care should be taken to ensure that it is never abused. Physical restraint should never be used as a punishment or to force a student to comply with a request. A student should not be restrained longer than the time needed to establish safety. Physical restraint has the potential to erupt into a power struggle between the restrainer and the student. Team members may wish to observe one another to ensure that this does not happen.

As with all strategies, be sure that consequences are age-appropriate, respectful, and appropriate for inclusive settings. These are minimum criteria for facilitating inclusion without stigmatizing or humiliating the student.

Long-Term Supports

Advantages

This fourth component of a comprehensive behavior support plan consists of two approaches, both geared toward the long-term prevention of problem behaviors, *lifestyle interventions,* and *maintenance and generalization strategies.*

Lifestyle interventions contribute to the long-term prevention of problem behaviors through the general improvement of the person's quality of life. Lifestyle refers to the rhythm and routines of daily life—where one lives, goes to school, and recreates; what goes on in those settings; how things are accomplished and with whom; and how activities contribute to personal satisfaction and enjoyment. Although presented in the last component in this book, an individual's lifestyle is often the first consideration made by a team, because one's lifestyle provides the context for all supportive efforts.

There are at least two important reasons for considering lifestyle interventions. First, a student's poor quality of life (e.g., limited opportunities for choice and control, loneliness, exclusion) or dissatisfaction with daily events may contribute directly to problem behavior. In fact, it may be the heart of the problem. No matter how well intentioned the other intervention components are, they may not produce positive outcomes if lifestyle factors are not addressed.

For example, providing a choice of activities, teaching an alternative skill for signaling a "break," and reinforcing good working habits are not likely to produce positive results for a student who is extremely dissatisfied with a vocational program that insists on training him for assembly jobs if he has no interest in such work. These interventions may make work a little more tolerable, but the bigger picture, being forced into a disliked vocation that he does not enjoy, is missed.

Second, students are more likely to learn acceptable social behaviors in contexts that are enjoyable, important, and meaningful to them. Students with a history of problem behaviors are routinely denied access to typical school, community, and, sometimes, home activities. The longer problem behavior persists, the more intrusive interventions may become. The more intrusive the intervention, the less opportunity the person has for choice and control, and the more likely the student is to be segregated from typical activities. A critical goal is to reverse this negative cycle by building supportive contexts in inclusive settings.

• •

Meaningful community participation and inclusion are promoted when lifestyle interventions are included in behavior support plans.

—Kincaid, Knoster, Harrower, Shannon, & Bustamante, 2002; Turnbull & Turnbull, 1999

Maintenance and generalization strategies allow for ongoing, long-term support of the individual. Students' personal needs as well as school, home, and community environments are constantly changing. Many students with disabilities need continued assistance to maintain alternative skills, apply them in different situations, and learn additional skills for new situations. Furthermore, ongoing team support may be needed to build supportive social contexts that are both accepting of students with disabilities and responsive to their needs.

Strategies

Long-term support strategies are less systematic than other interventions. Teams should brainstorm strategies and match interventions to school, home, and community settings based on an assessment of daily routines, available resources, student preferences, and family priorities. Teams are encouraged to consider structured person-centered planning processes for this purpose. Several resources are listed in the Bibliography (Appendix E).

At a minimum, consider two important guiding questions in your planning. *What lifestyle factors can be improved that will result in a personally gratifying quality of life for the student?* To answer, refer back to your global hypothesis for the student. Specifically, consider discrepancies between the individual's daily routines and those of peers without disabilities or discrepancies between the person's current activities and her preferences. In addition, consider what lifestyle factors appear to be contributing to problem behavior. Consider the quality of relationships among friends and family; opportunities for choice and control; opportunities to engage in meaningful, preferred activities; and inclusion in typical school and community activities. Also consider the student's general health and well-being.

After making these considerations, ask, "What can we do?" Generate short-term and long-term goals. Identify a "now" list for actions that can help the student and family realize immediate lifestyle improvements. Also consider long-term actions that may take a year or more to develop. See Table 13 on the next page for several examples of lifestyle interventions and supports.

Some teams wonder how it is possible to facilitate lifestyle changes for the student in settings outside of school, such as the home. Family partnerships are critical in this regard. Team members involving family can collaborate on interventions that can be tried at home. School professionals can help families connect with other needed resources and child-serving agencies (e.g., after-school buddy programs, in-home behavioral support, family counseling). Furthermore, some problem situations occurring in other settings can be mitigated

TABLE 13

Long-Term Supports

Types of intervention	Examples
Lifestyle changes ■ Relationships ■ Choice and control ■ Preferred activities ■ Inclusion ■ Health and well-being	1. Help the student maintain friendships by inviting peers to play and share in common interests. 2. Use peer networks to introduce the student into play groups. 3. Incorporate opportunities for daily choice making in all routines. 4. Develop an action plan that will move the student from a segregated to an inclusionary school setting. 5. Sample prospective jobs; help the individual to procure his choice. 6. Arrange school schedule to provide periods of rest during the day.
Maintenance/ Generalization strategies ■ Extended skill training ■ Prepare others ■ Permanent accommodations	1. Teach teachers and staff in other settings how to make specific accommodations. 2. Teach teachers, staff, and family members to reinforce use of alternative skills over time and in other settings. 3. Teach peers to understand the individual's communication system. 4. Use picture schedules to make daily routines predictable and understandable to the student. 5. Help the student practice and praise the use of new skills in different settings. 6. Develop the student's problem-solving skills. 7. Help the student set and monitor goals.

in school. For example, extra time to complete homework assignments can be built into the student's school day. Opportunities to shower in the school locker room can help the student address matters of personal hygiene.

There is a second question to consider in your planning: *What supports are needed to maintain positive student outcomes in all applicable settings?* Maintenance and generalization strategies include extended skill training to help the student apply alternative skills in new situations and settings and maintain their use over time. For example, you might come up with a plan to teach the student how to use alternative skills in multiple school settings or how to use a cue card to remind himself to take five when frustrated. This card can then be carried to various settings. Self-monitoring and picture cue checklists are also useful for helping students generalize and maintain new skills. For instance, Quinn uses a picture checklist to remind him how to organize his work materials. He brings it with him to other classes. As Quinn uses his picture checklist across environments, he experiences success and teacher praise across settings, which in turn contributes to the maintenance and generalization of skills.

Sometimes students revert back to their problem behaviors because not all relevant adults or other students know how to respond to their communication attempts or know about key elements of their behavior support plan. Thus preparing others to support the student is also important in helping the student maintain and generalize new skills. Do others know how to prevent problem behaviors? Are they responding in ways that reinforce the student to use alternative skills? Do they know what to do to avert a crisis?

Finally, consider identifying permanent accommodations for the student as a third way of helping students maintain and generalize positive outcomes. As discussed earlier, some antecedent modifications can become permanent accommodations when they are needed by the student to function or participate in daily activities. Be sure these permanent accommodations are documented in the student's IEP and other instructional plans to ensure that they will be implemented and carried over year to year. See Table 13 for examples of strategies to promote maintenance and generalization.

• •

Elena

The team referred back to Elena's global hypothesis and broad assessments. Elena's lack of participation in typical school activities and limited opportunities for peer interaction were the most important lifestyle factors to address. Elena had been placed in a self-contained classroom because of her severe disabilities and history of self-injury. The team soon recognized that this placement was counterproductive to Elena's long-term goals. The team speculated that the underlying reason for Elena's frequent demand for teacher attention was that she had neither the skills nor the opportunity to do much of anything else when not participating in teacher-led activities. Elena was a social child who liked being active. Although the team had targeted alternative social and communicative skills, the current classroom situation provided little opportunity for her to learn or maintain new skills. It did not provide the rich opportunities for social interaction, activity participation, and play available in general education settings.

The first lifestyle goal was to get Elena involved in the school's Friendship Club, bringing her into school social activities. A year ago Elena was considered a poor candidate for this program because of her tendency toward self-injury. Now, with a better understanding of the reasons for Elena's self-injury, the team is far less apprehensive. Elena's support plan arranges for same-aged peers from general education classrooms to interact with Elena during club meetings, outside recess, lunch, free play, art, and other social activities. In addition, peers are to participate in Elena's class, as well as invite her to participate in their class activities. These social situations will serve as excellent contexts for teaching targeted social and communication skills, facilitating friendships, and discovering new activities that Elena enjoys.

As Elena increases her participation in school activities, peers and other teachers must understand how Elena communicates. To help Elena maintain and generalize her alternative communication skills, another goal is to teach peers and teachers (a) how to initiate interactions in ways Elena can understand and (b) how to respond to Elena's communication, her use of a picture book and nonverbal gestures.

For a second long-term lifestyle goal, the team targeted inclusion in a general education class, seeing this as the best way to ensure consistent participation in regular school activities. This requires long-range planning with general education teachers and administrators.

Looking toward this second long-term goal, the team considered ways of expanding and building on Elena's alternative skills. Hand raising, making simple requests by means of a communication book, and taking turns during play activities were important but only rudimentary social skills. More sophisticated skills were needed to participate in a variety of settings. Tentative plans included teaching Elena alternative ways of gaining teacher attention (e.g., approaching the teacher, arm tapping) and how to choose and initiate both independent and social play activities. To enhance communication, the team also planned to explore augmentative communication devices. Observing Elena in the context of typical school activities will provide ideas for future goals.

Summary

PBS plans are uniquely tailored to each individual's needs, preferences, and long-range goals. Long-term effectiveness is a result of multiple components working together to address a student's complex needs. In this chapter we described the purpose, advantages, and limitations of four intervention components that make up a comprehensive behavior support plan. We also provided guiding questions, considerations, and multiple examples to support your team's planning efforts. By way of a self-checklist, we have summarized key points and outcomes for designing comprehensive support plans (see Table 14).

TABLE 14

Self-Check for Designing Comprehensive Support Plans

Antecedent and setting-event modifications

Does the plan include antecedent and setting-event modifications to prevent problem behavior from occurring?	Y	N
Does the plan include modifications to make desired behaviors more likely?	Y	N

Teaching alternative skills

Did your team consider all three approaches to alternative-skill training (e.g., replacement skills, general skills, coping skills)?	Y	N
Do replacement skills serve the same function as the problem behavior?	Y	N
Do general skills help the student prevent problem situations from occurring?	Y	N
If the plan targets multiple alternative skills, are the ones that produce the most immediate effect for the student taught first?	Y	N

Consequence interventions

Does the plan include consequence strategies for (a) strengthening alternative skills, (b) reducing the payoff for problem behavior, and (c) crisis management if necessary?	Y	N
Do consequences for alternative skills produce outcomes that are more effective or efficient than the problem behavior?	Y	N
Are desired outcomes for the problem behavior reduced or eliminated?	Y	N

Does the crisis management plan address the three phases of a crisis: (a) escalation, (b) eruption, and (c) de-escalation?	Y	N

Long-term supports

Does the plan include lifestyle changes that will improve the student's quality of life?	Y	N
Does the plan include strategies that will help the student maintain and generalize skills to new situations?	Y	N

Overall

Are the intervention strategies logically linked to the specific and global hypotheses?	Y	N
Does the plan reflect student and family preferences?	Y	N
Are all the intervention strategies (a) age-appropriate and (b) acceptable for other students without disabilities?	Y	N
Can the plan be carried out in everyday settings without stigmatizing the student?	Y	N

CHAPTER 4

Measuring Progress and Making Changes

S upport plans are effective when they produce meaningful outcomes. Luanna Meyer and colleagues were among the first to define meaningful outcomes as results that are important to the student, family, school, and community. Because problem behaviors can significantly interfere with an individual's quality of life (e.g., relationships, access to preferred activities, inclusion), effectiveness must be evaluated in terms of personally meaningful results.

Meaningful outcomes should reflect (a) increases in the use of new alternative skills, (b) decreases in the incidence of problem behavior, and (c) general improvements in lifestyle or quality of life. As such, it is important that your team evaluate progress

- to see if new skills are being learned;

- to assess whether new skills are used across different situations;

- to see if the problem behavior is decreasing at an acceptable rate;

- to see if the student and his family's quality of life (as viewed from their perspective) has improved;

- to assess student, teacher, and parent satisfaction with the plan and its outcomes;

- to adapt and modify the plan as needed.

When evaluating the effectiveness of a support plan, consider three important questions: (a) *What type of information do you need to gather?* (b) *How will you and your team collect this information?* (c) *How will your team use the information to make decisions?*

. . . .

Is the support plan working? Effectiveness is evaluated by measuring
multiple, meaningful outcomes for the student, school, and family.

—Meyer & Janney, 1989

What and How to Measure

Your team will need to consider collecting many kinds of information by any number of means. Table 15 summarizes both "what" and "how" to collect outcome information.

Deciding what information to collect and measure will be guided by the goals in your student's support plan, with the most obvious being (a) the increase in use of alternative skills (replacement skills, general skills, and coping skills) and (b) the reduction in occurrence of problem behavior. Teams may want to monitor these outcomes over time and across different situations (e.g., in different classrooms, in the community, at home). You will also want to measure broader results such as those related to lifestyle interventions and supports. This might include measuring positive side effects of support (e.g., improved grades or increased class participation); improvements in health (e.g., decreases in psychotropic medications, fewer bruises); and student, family, or staff satisfaction with the executed plan. Quality-of-life measures may reflect increased participation in typical school activities, increased opportunities for age-appropriate choice and control, and improved relationships with others.

The best collecting and measuring methods will provide the most useful information for decision making without interfering in typical school or home routines. As shown in Table 15, teams may consider a variety of methods for collecting information. Direct observation, involving frequency counts or rate measures, is well suited to evaluating reductions in problem behavior and increases in the use of new skills in classroom settings. More indirect methods, such as communication logs, may be better suited for home and general education settings. Broader outcomes, such as improvements in quality of life, health, or consumer satisfaction, may be measured by a variety of means such as collecting data

TABLE 15
Measuring and Monitoring Progress

What information to collect

- Increases in use of alternative skills

- Reductions in occurrence of problem behavior

- Positive side effects (e.g., improved grades, increased attention, peer acceptance)

- Improvements in quality of life (e.g., increased participation in typical activities, increased choice/decision making, inclusion)

- Improvements in consumer satisfaction (e.g., student, family, staff, and others)

- Improvements in health or well-being

How to collect information

- Interviews (e.g., teachers, students, parents, service providers)

- Informal and anecdotal reports (e.g., communication logs with parents, teacher progress notes)

- Rating scales (e.g., student effect, social scales, opportunities for choice)

- Natural documents (e.g., report cards, incident reports, medical records, placement records)

- Direct observation (e.g., frequency counts, measures of duration, observation logs)

Adapted from Meyer and Janney (1989).

from "natural" school documents (e.g., report cards, placement records, minutes from meetings) and typical student assessments (e.g., social rating scales, progress notes). Before selecting methods, ask what forms of documentation are already in your setting and how your team might use them to gather information.

In addition to determining what to collect and how to collect it, your team will need to identify who will take the lead in gathering information. In particular, your team should answer the following four questions:

1. Who will collect what pieces of information and in which settings?

2. Who will be responsible for summarizing and displaying the information?

3. When and how often will information be collected?

4. Who will meet, when, and how often to review and discuss the displayed information for decision making?

Elena

To illustrate, see Elena's progress evaluation plan in Appendix C. In this plan, Elena's team identified three specific assessment areas: decreases in problem behavior, increases in alternative skills, and improvements in quality of life. The team selected a variety of measures to evaluate effectiveness. Staff members most directly involved with a problem incident record each incident in a log. These records are summarized at the end of each week by Mrs. Gallago to determine whether problem behavior is decreasing across all school settings. Frequency counts are also used to evaluate Elena's acquisition of alternative skills. These measures are taken by Mrs. Gallago or the teacher assistant during instructional situations. More indirect measures, such as weekly communication logs with home and progress notes made by other teachers, are used to evaluate Elena's spontaneous use of her new skills across school and home settings. To evaluate improvements in Elena's social interaction skills, Mrs. Gallago agreed to observe Elena at least once a week in a social play situation and anecdotally record her observations in a narrative log.

Whenever possible, measures to evaluate improvements in Elena's quality of life made use of natural school assessments and documents. Increased participation in social activities at school will be evaluated by recording Elena's weekly social activities and by keeping a record of the Friendship Club's activity schedule. Informal discussions with and progress reports made by general education teachers and parents will provide further information on Elena's participation in social activities and her interactions with peers; they also indicate parental and teacher consumer satisfaction. Finally, to evaluate progress toward placing Elena in a general education classroom, the team will keep a record of their planning efforts and official documents (e.g., minutes of meetings, action plan, letters, placement records).

Monitoring Progress

While reaching agreement on what type of information to collect and how to collect it is important, understanding how to make program decisions using this information is critical for long-term success. Based on the information you collect, your team will need to determine whether to reevaluate components of the plan or strengthen support strategies, or when to expand the plan beyond its current scope.

When the support plan is effective, your team will realize increases in new skills, reductions in problem behavior, and progress toward broader lifestyle improvements. When this happens, your team should ask, What's next? Do these gains justify maintaining the status quo, or should the support plan be expanded to enhance further growth?

If progress is not sufficient, your team should ask, Why not? It may be that your team's hypotheses are inaccurate or that the plan does not adequately address the influences or function of the student's problem behavior. Perhaps the plan was implemented inappropriately, or other events hindered positive outcomes. Lack of sufficient progress should result in teams reevaluating and modifying support plan components, rather than considering more restrictive interventions or placements.

Making decisions about the effectiveness of a support plan requires thoughtful consideration. Keep in mind that modifications are likely as a person's needs and circumstances change over time. As you evaluate progress, your team is encouraged to consider the questions in Table 16 to troubleshoot problems with the support plan's effectiveness.

Summary

Collaborating as a team is the best approach to evaluating progress and making modifications to support plans. Reaching consensus on establishing meaningful outcomes with the student and his or her family is required throughout the process. Considering all relevant forms of information is also important. Listening and respecting the student's and family's perspectives, in tandem with defining how information is to be collected and used in decision making, will best ensure the realization of expected outcomes.

TABLE 16
Troubleshooting Insufficient Progress

Considerations	Team action
Have you provided sufficient time for the support plan to take effect?	■ Review timeline ■ Provide more time if needed
Are support plan interventions linked to the hypotheses for problem behavior?	■ Review interventions to determine how they address setting events, antecedents, and function of problem behavior ■ Revise if necessary
Is the support plan being implemented as planned?	■ Observe to see whether interventions are implemented ■ Hold team discussions; ask, Do you need help? Is it doable in your setting? What else can we do? ■ If necessary, offer team members training or modify interventions to fit their setting and skills
Are your hypotheses still relevant? Could something have changed for the student?	■ Review your functional assessment data; consider whether the data are still relevant ■ Collect more assessment information if necessary; revise hypotheses
Are your interventions sufficiently effective?	■ Consider whether all triggers for problem behaviors are addressed by antecedent interventions ■ Consider whether alternative skills are effective and efficient for the student. From the student's perspective, do they bring about desired results? ■ Consider whether reinforcing consequences for alternative skills need to be strengthened
Has the plan sufficiently addressed student preferences and quality of life? Are you addressing the big picture?	■ Consider whether there has been recent life or health changes for the student ■ Review plan to assess student satisfaction with his/her curriculum, school, and social activities ■ Revise plan to reflect student/family goals and preferences

CHAPTER 5

Practical Considerations

D esigning positive behavior support (PBS) plans as described
in earlier chapters is a process that emphasizes strategies and
supports for prevention (antecedent/setting-event modifications), teaching (teaching alternative skills), and responding to behavior
(consequence interventions). The process begins with a comprehensive
functional behavior assessment (FBA) that typically involves direct
observations and results in a support plan with multiple components.
Often comprehensive support plans are designed across multiple settings and are longitudinal in nature. The process, as previously described, can seem overwhelming because of the various component
parts of support plans coupled with practical realities associated with
designing and implementing them. One of the more commonly voiced
concerns about the PBS process is the concern about time constraints.
The amount of time (and energy) required to both design and implement support plans will vary from team to team and from situation to
situation. Certainly, the more complex the student's situation, the more
comprehensive the support plan and, subsequently, the greater the time
and effort required to design and implement the plan. However, finding
the resources even under the most complex circumstances represents
a good investment of time.

One way to minimize the amount of time required to design and implement a support plan is through early intervention. In short, the sooner
the process is applied in response to increasing levels of problem behavior, the more time efficient (and manageable) designing behavior support plans become. Time efficiency is directly related to the "doability"
of any given support plan. Elena's example has been selected to illustrate

the process of designing a comprehensive support plan. However, the application of the comprehensive process described in the example may not always be required of all support teams. In other words, there are ways in which the process can be abridged through early intervention. Teams are encouraged to take into account the considerations listed in Table 17 in order to determine whether an abridged or a comprehensive approach is required to design a positive behavior support plan.

T A B L E   1 7

Guiding Questions and Considerations for Selecting an Abridged vs. a Comprehensive PBS Process

Guiding questions	Consideration of the abridged process	Consideration of the comprehensive process
Is this the first attempt by the team to design a support plan for this individual?	The abridged process may be relevant if this is the first attempt at designing a support plan for an individual student. However, the responses to the remaining Guiding Questions are relevant before a decision to start with the abridged process is reached.	A comprehensive process may be required only if this is not the first attempt at designing a support plan for an individual student. This may be the case where numerous support plans have been tried with less than desired results.
Has the level of problem behavior with this individual, although difficult and concerning, been manageable or has there been need for crisis intervention in response to serious destructive behavior?	The abridged process may be relevant if the level of problem behavior has not warranted crisis intervention to protect the individual or others from harm and/or to prevent significant property damage.	A comprehensive process may be required if the frequency, duration, and/or intensity of the problem behavior has required crisis intervention to protect the individual or others from harm and/or to prevent significant property damage.

Has an initial FBA been conducted with the results summarized into hypothesis statements?	The abridged process may be relevant if this is the team's first (or an early) attempt at conducting an FBA.	A comprehensive process may be required if this is not the first attempt at conducting an FBA.
Is the problem behavior of concern present in multiple contexts, or is it somewhat isolated in one or two situations?	The abridged process may be relevant if the problem behavior appears limited to one or two particular situations (e.g., two activities within a classroom).	A comprehensive process may be required if the problem behavior appears to be present across multiple situations or settings (e.g., at home, in the community and at school, or across multiple contexts at school).

Abridging the Process

Abridging the process (when appropriate) to gather information and develop a behavior support plan can save time and resources. However, abridging the process does not mean deviating from the operating set of assumptions or essential principles of practice associated with providing positive behavior support as highlighted with Elena. Rather, in an abridged approach, the scope of the functional assessment process becomes more narrowly defined by the greatest emphasis having been placed on measures that lead to developing a specific hypothesis. Typically, the hypothesis that emerges as a result of an abridged FBA process is limited to a particular context (e.g., in the classroom at school) or situation within a particular setting (e.g., writing activities in the classroom). As a result, the subsequent support plan may include antecedent/setting-event modifications, teaching alternative skills, or consequence interventions that are limited to just those few contexts in which the problem behavior occurs. More complex assessment procedures that span across multiple life domains—such as person-centered planning that can lead to more comprehensive long-term supports as previously described with Elena—are reserved for the more comprehensive process of providing positive behavior support. For comparative purposes, examples of component parts of a support plan that was developed as a result of the abridged PBS process for Carl (a young boy in fifth grade diagnosed with Asperger's syndrome) is provided in Appendix D. There are two significant differences between the more comprehensive approach (Elena, Appendix B) and an abridged PBS process. First, only a specific hypothesis is generated in the abridged FBA process, and second, as a result of the more narrowly focused FBA, long-term supports, especially lifestyle interventions, are typically omitted from an abridged support plan. Because the abridged process does not focus on destructive behaviors, a crisis management plan is typically not included. A more comprehensive application of the PBS process (both FBA and design of the support plan) is recommended in instances where the individual does not sufficiently respond to implementation of a support plan that has been developed through the abridged process. In such cases, a more comprehensive assessment may be warranted.

Abridging the Functional Behavioral Assessment

Emphasis in the abridged process of gathering information is placed on gathering specific information that will be limited in scope to the immediacy of the environment within which the problem behavior occurs. Many teams may find that indirect measures (e.g., team discussions, interviews, and other informant methods) are sufficient for developing workable specific hypotheses. Team members who (through reflection) are effective observers may find convergence (agreement) with regard to the specific triggers and function of the student's problem behavior relying only on indirect measures. However, direct observation may be required when there appears to be a lack of convergence of perspectives among team members. It is possible to create one useful specific hypothesis statement in the course of one team meeting in the instance where convergence between team members is present. Important questions to answer when conducting an FBA were highlighted in chapter 2 (see Table 4, Gather Specific Information). These same questions are relevant to conducting an FBA through the abridged process. The specific information gathered is then summarized into a specific hypothesis, also described in chapter 2. Figure 5 provides an example of a specific hypothesis, developed by a team conducting an abridged FBA for Carl.

FIGURE 5
Specific Hypothesis for Carl

When this happens:

Carl is directed to complete tasks that involve fifth-grade-level reading (particularly in science and social studies) or when he feels confused by directions (particularly written directions) to the point where he thinks he will not succeed in accurately completing an assigned academic task while in the presence of his peers in group settings.

Carl does this:

makes derogatory statements about the teacher or work, gets out of his seat, and refuses to do the work.

In order to:

escape the undesired task and/or avoid appearing "stupid" in front of his classmates.

Abridging the Support Plan

In a compatible manner with comprehensive support plans such as Elena's, emphasis in a support plan developed through the abridged process identifies procedures for antecedent/setting-event modifications, teaching alternative skills and consequence interventions. However, unlike a support plan developed through a more comprehensive approach, a support plan developed through the abridged process typically does not reflect comprehensive long-term supports or crisis management. Furthermore, support plans developed through the abridged process may focus on only a few alternative skills and will more than likely be limited in application to a particular context (situation) as opposed to multiple contexts (e.g., in the classroom at school as opposed to a support plan for use at home and school as well as in the community). Priority in the abridged process continues to be placed on (a) addressing the triggers that appear to lead to problem behavior in order to prevent problem behavior, (b) teaching socially acceptable alternative skills (most often focusing on general and coping skills), and (c) ways in which to respond to future occurrence of both appropriate and problem behavior. In general, the nature of an individual's problem behavior does not usually warrant the crisis management component of a support plan in instances where the abridged process has been employed by a team. Teams are encouraged to carefully consider the guiding questions noted in Table 17 to determine if it is appropriate to abridge the support plan process.

A Good Place to Start

Whether designing an abridged or comprehensive behavior support plan, a good place to start in the planning process is by focusing initially on the immediate needs of members of the support team. By definition, problem behaviors are challenging to team members. So, in addition to prioritizing around the student's needs, it's important to prioritize around team needs as well, by asking, *What do we need in order to be successful?* Often it is necessary to address the immediate needs of team members in order to gain trust and solidify commitment among the team members to the PBS process. While no universal list of supports for team members exists, there are a number of logical types of supports to take into consideration at the onset of designing the support plan. Examples of supports that surface during the design phase are (a) creating a series of scheduled team meetings, (b) arranging for consults with other service providers (including medical doctors when relevant), and (c) addressing informational and professional development needs of individual team members. The bottom line is that the likelihood of successful design and implementation of a behavior support may be directly related to the degree to which members of the support team believe their needs are equally being addressed.

It is also logical at the onset of designing a support plan to focus on what a good day would look like (from the perspective of team members) for the student of concern. In other words, what would the ideal ebb and flow of the individual's day look like for him or her to be successful? Using this frame of reference can greatly assist support teams

as they design initial prevention, teaching, and responding strategies into the support plan. By focusing on what needs to be in place in order to have a successful day, team members are creating contexts where both the student and staff can immediately experience success. Such an approach can facilitate team camaraderie and motivation to continue to work through problems. For example, Carl has very poor reading skills. In fact, one trigger that leads to problem behavior as noted in his specific hypothesis is when he is directed to complete tasks that require fifth-grade-level reading. As such, a good day (from Carl's as well as the team's perspective) would likely include Carl being asked to complete tasks at his instructional third-grade reading level as opposed to being asked to complete academic tasks (e.g., social studies and science) that require him to read assignments that are not at his instructional level (in Carl's case, fifth-grade-level reading). Using this "good day" as a common frame of reference can help the support team to clearly focus on strategies and supports that will likely have a fast, positive impact (for further examples of interventions for Carl, see Appendix D).

Once the initial behavior support plan has been designed, implementation of the plan becomes the focal point for the support team. Teams are encouraged to prioritize aspects of the behavior support plan that directly address what the members of the team view as the most pressing problem(s). In a practical sense, this means that not all component parts of a given support plan need to be emphasized or implemented at the same time. In this regard, the team should initially select strategies that they believe will bring about quick, positive change. For example, often teams initially implement antecedent/setting-event modifications first in order to establish greater opportunities over time within which to teach new alternative skills (replacement, general, and/or coping skills).

It is therefore essential that members of the support team reach consensus on both (a) what they view as the most immediate pressing concern and (b) what components or intervention strategies to initiate first in order to address those most immediate pressing concerns. In the instance where a comprehensive support plan is being designed, it is likely that the team will need to place greatest emphasis on both antecedent and setting-event modifications (short-term prevention) and crisis management as described in the previous chapters.

Behavior support plans (whether abridged or comprehensive) are about addressing needs that include those of both the student and the team members (e.g., teachers, family members, peers). It is important to keep in mind that any given support plan (even when effective) should change at some point as needs change over time. Sometimes the need arises to change aspects of a given support plan sooner rather than later as a result of insufficient progress. At other times a support plan may continue to be implemented in its current form for an extended period of time when it appears that all aspects of the support plan are having the desired effect (reductions in problem behavior, increases in the acquisition and use of alternative skills, improved quality of life). All support plans evolve over time as needs and circumstances change for the individual as well as the support team.

The operating assumptions and guiding principles for both the abridged and the comprehensive approach to designing support plans are essentially one in the same. The subtle differences between the two highlight how the processes differ in terms of scope and component parts relative to designing support plans. As stated earlier, the fundamental point to understand is that both of these processes are consistent with one another as each reflects to the guiding principles of designing effective PBS plans. The abridged process may be relevant for a given team based on less complicated circumstances as denoted in Table 17. However, a more comprehensive application of the PBS process as described in the previous chapters (both FBA and design of the support plan) is recommended in instances where the individual does not sufficiently respond to a support plan that has been developed through the abridged process.

CHAPTER 6

Commonly Asked Questions

Our purpose for this book is to provide a conceptual framework for understanding, designing, and evaluating positive behavior support (PBS) plans for individuals with developmental disabilities who engage in problem behaviors. As emphasized, PBS is an assessment-based, problem-solving process that involves teams selecting intervention and support options that best address individual needs within the context of everyday school, home, and community settings. In previous chapters we offered guiding questions and considerations that teams will find helpful in designing effective and meaningful supports. Unfortunately, no book by itself can address all concerns. Acknowledging this, we provide some brief responses to a few additional commonly asked questions about individualized positive behavior support plans.

Developing positive behavior support plans as you have described in this book appears to reflect a very different approach than what we currently do at my school...where do I start?

While the PBS approach described in this book does not reflect a brand new approach in the field, unfortunately it is not uncommon to find some staff in schools who view positive behavior support as a dramatic change in practice. Therefore, it is important to thoughtfully initiate discussion and collaborative activities related to individualized positive behavior support in your school. It may prove most helpful to try to initiate application of the PBS process through an abridged application (such as Carl's) as opposed to starting out with a student whose situation warrants a more comprehensive application of the PBS process (such as

Elena). This should ideally position your initial student-centered team to most effectively "learn as you go" with a greater likelihood of experiencing quick success as a result of sufficient student progress. However, in the instance where you are compelled to start with a situation that requires a comprehensive approach you are encouraged to consider initially focusing on what an ideal day might look like as highlighted in chapter 5. In all cases, seeking support through your building principal is essential for sustaining individualized PBS activities.

· ·

How long does it take to complete a functional assessment?

As described in chapter 5, the time required to complete an abridged FBA will likely be considerably less than the time required to complete a more comprehensive FBA. In either case, there will likely be a relationship between your team's familiarity with the student of concern and the amount of time necessary to complete an adequate FBA. As such, there is no single answer to this question. For teams who know the student well, an abridged functional assessment may take as little time as one or two meetings. However, the data gathering process may take weeks for teams just beginning to get to know the student or when conducting a more comprehensive FBA. It is important to point out that reaching an understanding about an individual, the contextual influences on behavior, and the function of the problem behavior is an ongoing process. After an initial assessment, once supports are implemented and evaluated, new assessment information is revealed. Expect to gather new information and reformulate your hypotheses as you continue to work with a student.

· ·

What if my team can't figure out the function of the problem behavior or all of the environmental influences?

Logically, teams struggling with identifying function or triggers to problem behavior as a result of conducting an abridged FBA are encouraged to conduct a more comprehensive FBA. Typically, teams can determine both the functional and environmental influences of an individual's problem behavior provided they stay focused and committed to the process of conducting a comprehensive assessment. However, under-standing the influences on problem behavior involves detective work. It takes time to problem solve, and it is usually impossible to find all the pieces of the puzzle all at once. If your team is struggling to gain a comprehensive understanding, we recommend designing support plans around the information you do feel confident about (what you know). Often this means modifying some known antecedent variables as you continue to gain a greater understanding of the function or purpose of the problem behavior. Once supports are implemented, observe and collect new information to broaden your hypotheses. As we indicated in the question above, functional assessment is ongoing. Teams will gain new insight about the students' problem behaviors once they imple-ment interventions based on what they currently know. Evaluating what interventions work or do not work will provide critical information for solving the assessment puzzle. Teams that continue to struggle might benefit from technical assistance from an external source.

• •

Are positive behavior support plans useful for students with other disabilities or significant mental health needs?

Yes, they can be. Elena was an example of a student with significant cognitive delays and autism where Carl was a student with Asperger's syndrome; however, the process is applicable for any individual who presents challenging behavior. For example, for students with learning disabilities, antecedent modifications may focus on curriculum or in-structional methods within the general education classroom. Alternative skills training may focus on teaching complex social interaction skills, problem solving, and organizational skills within typical school and community settings. Consequence interventions may directly involve the student in self-evaluation and self-monitoring across a variety of locations and situations.

When the student of concern has significant mental health needs, it may be important to include mental health professionals on the team. Even in cases where an individual's problem behavior is biologically based, teams can identify environmental influences that contribute to problem behaviors. Support plans may call for stress-reducing anteced-ent or long-term prevention that will help the person avoid or cope with difficult situations. In addition, for individuals with significant mental health needs, the FBA and support plan process may also be embedded within a person-centered planning or wraparound process as previously described.

• •

Is the PBS process applicable to home and community settings?

Yes. We chose to focus our book on school settings; however, the process for designing support plans can be used for any individual in any setting—home, community, work, and so forth. In fact, research shows that the same process can be successfully used for students without disabilities as well. Of course, in order for the support plan to have a good contextual fit, the process will have to be adapted to the settings in which the plan will be applied. The Resource Bibliography at the end of this book (Appendix E) provides a wealth of illustrative examples on how PBS support plans can be developed for other settings including in the home.

• •

How long should my team wait before modifying strategies or consid-ering a more restrictive placement?

There are no fixed time limits for judging a sufficient level of success (even though most would agree the sooner the better). As your team monitors progress, you will need to reach consensus on a reasonable time frame for evaluating the degree of behavior change. If goals are not being realized in a reasonable amount of time, we see moving toward a more restrictive placement without exhausting all possible options as a misguided decision. The focus should be on finding modifications that can be made to support the individual within current or less restrictive settings. Very few interventions cannot be made portable to integrated settings. When goals are not being sufficiently realized, ask two ques-tions: What modifications on our part are needed for success? What can we do to make these changes happen?

How does the restrictiveness of a student's educational placement affect positive behavior support plans?

PBS plans can be implemented with a variety of individuals and across settings (e.g., across the continuum of educational placement options available in schools). However, restrictiveness of educational placement may influence a number of student-specific factors that will need to be addressed by the team. For example, difficulties in achieving both short- and long-term behavior change may arise if the student is interested in community-based employment; however, his educational placement is in a self-contained workshop environment doing factory line assembly designed exclusively for students with disabilities. In another example, a fourth-grade student might be more likely to rebel (through problem behavior) if she is interested in doing the type of curricular and social activities that her same-age peers are doing in the third-grade classroom while she is restricted to a curriculum focusing on pre-academic tasks in a self-contained special education classroom. The PBS process in both of these examples may be applied with varying degrees of success; however, the degree and durability of positive behavior change realized in such examples may be limited due to the adverse impact of more restrictive placements on each student's motivation. In both of these examples the students' interests reflect program aspects that are different from what may typically be available in both of these more restrictive educational placements. Teams are encouraged to consider planning transitions into more normative or inclusive settings in cases where a positive behavior support plan is initially designed to be implemented with students in more restrictive settings.

What do you do when the student is frequently in crisis?

Repeated use of a crisis management component of a behavior support plan signals the need to (a) reassess the team's hypotheses, (b) modify or change interventions and supports, and/or (c) expand the focus or aspects of the support plan. Keep in mind that the problem behavior serves a function for the student. High levels of crisis clearly indicate that something in your team's plan isn't working. The team should specifically look at how it can strengthen or modify all other components of the support plan (antecedent or setting-event strategies, teaching alternative skills including reinforcement procedures, long-term supports) and ensure that the team includes all the relevant people (students with the most complex needs often require an interagency team and may benefit from person-centered planning procedures). During crisis a team's first response is to react and protect. However, no matter how difficult the situation, teams must stay focused on problem solving to achieve durable, long-term outcomes.

● ●

Are all components of a positive support plan necessary?

Positive behavior support is a system in which each component contributes to long-term effectiveness and meaningful outcomes. In chapter 5 we provided considerations and distinctions between component parts of a comprehensive behavior support plan (Elena) and a support plan developed through an abridged process (Carl). Whether abridged or comprehensive in nature, each component should be considered; however, recognize that not all components may carry equal weight for every individual and that different components may be more heavily emphasized at different times. Just as the lives of people are complex and dynamic, so too is the process of providing individualized positive behavior support.

● ●

How do I balance implementing a support plan for one student with the needs of the other students in my classroom?

This is often a common concern for teachers, but in reality, implementing individualized behavior support plans is no more complicated than implementing other individualized accommodations or supports for students with disabilities in other areas such as academics. Teachers may also find that accommodations made for one student may benefit the whole class. We know one creative teacher, for example, who, when faced with a child who frequently blurted out irrelevant statements during whole group activities, implemented a classwide intervention plan to address this child's needs. She set clear expectations for hand raising and initiated a class competition for thoughtful responses to her questions. Not only did the student's behavior dramatically improve, but she discovered that her whole class became more engaged and thoughtful.

● ●

Our school has begun to implement schoolwide PBS. How does a positive behavior support plan for an individual student fit in with our whole school approach?

SWPBS initiatives typically begin with implementing primary (universal) prevention strategies involving the whole school and all students. The presence of SWPBS at primary (universal—for all students) as well as secondary (targeted group) prevention can serve as an excellent context to design and implement individualized behavior support plans (tertiary-level prevention). Because the entire school community is educated about basic PBS principles and practices, school personnel who are called to serve on a student-centered team will be familiar with basic preventive strategies and the importance of data collection for progress monitoring. Moreover, it is easier to implement individualized interventions in schools that have adopted good classroom management practices than it is in schools or classrooms that do not have preventive practices in place. When primary and secondary prevention strategies are in place, the number of students who require individualized behavior supports may be reduced. Still, although important, schoolwide or classwide strategies are not a panacea. There will always be some students who require an individualized approach as described in this book to address their unique needs.

・・・・・・・

APPENDIX A

Guiding Questions for Designing
Comprehensive Positive Behavior Support Plans

Antecedent and Setting-Event Modifications

- How can the triggering antecedent or setting events be changed so that problem situations can be prevented?

- What can be added to the student's daily routines to make desired behaviors more likely and situations more pleasant for the individual?

Teaching Alternative Skills

- When a problem situation arises, what alternative skill could the student use that would serve the same function as the problem behavior (replacement skill)?

- What general skills (e.g., social, communication, leisure, academic) might help the student prevent problem situations?

- What skills are needed to help the student cope with potentially difficult or frustrating situations that cannot or should not be changed (coping and tolerance)?

Consequence Interventions

- How will you reinforce the student's use of alternative skills so that they become more effective and efficient than the problem behavior?

- How will you teach the student that the problem behavior is no longer effective, efficient, or desirable?

- What can be done to de-escalate crisis situations and protect the student and others from harm?

Long-Term Supports

- What lifestyle factors could be improved for a personally more gratifying quality of life for the student?

- What supports are needed to maintain and generalize positive student outcomes in all settings?

• • • • • • • •

Elena's Behavior Support Plan

Antecedent and setting event modifications

Increase teacher interaction and activity participation during unstructured activities:

- stay in close proximity to Elena; increase turns;

- involve Elena in teacher activities;

- offer independent activities during down periods;

- modify schedule to reduce "alone" periods.

When Elena is sick, frequently check on her during all activities; offer opportunities for change of activities or rest.

Alternative skills

Replacement skill

- Teach hand raising to call for teacher attention.

General skills

- Teach "requesting" using a picture communication book.

- Teach social exchanges during play activities.

- Teach independent play skills.

Coping skill

- Teach tolerance for "waiting."

Consequence interventions

Increase use of alternative skills

- Respond immediately and consistently to Elena's hand raising.

- Use praise and natural consequences for social, play, and communication skills.

- Provide stickers for "waiting."

Reduce effectiveness of problem behavior

- Redirect Elena to raise her hand to use her communication book.

Crisis management

- Redirect as above.

- Hold Elena's hands, arms, and upper body till calm.

- Reintroduce to activities.

Long-term supports

Lifestyle interventions

- Use school Friendship Club to increase opportunities for social play and involvement in school activities.

- Develop a plan for further inclusion.

Maintenance/Generalization

- Teach peers and other teachers Elena's communication system.

- Teach other teachers to be responsive to nonverbal cues by reinforcing Elena's use of her alternative skills over time and across situations.

- Expand social and communication skills; focus on initiations and alternative ways of seeking adult assistance.

APPENDIX C

Progress Evaluation for Elena

Assessment area	Specific progress (What)	Measures (How, Who, How often)
Decreases in problem behavior	■ Decreased screaming, face slapping, and head banging in all school settings to near zero levels	■ Daily frequency counts recorded in incident logs (all instructional staff)
Increases in alternative skills	■ Raises hand to obtain teacher attention (replaces problem behavior) ■ Uses communication book to make simple requests ■ Plays independently with at least 3 activities ■ During social activities, shares materials and responds to other students' initiations ■ Can wait at least 10 minutes for teacher assistance	■ Daily frequency counts of hand raising, communication requests, and "waiting" during initial acquisition (Mrs. Gallago and assistant) ■ Document acquisition of independent play activities (Mrs. Gallago) ■ Weekly communication logs with home, report improvements in communication, independent play, and waiting (Mrs. Gallago, parents) ■ Observe social group (weekly), maintain progress notes (Mrs. Gallago, general education teacher)
Improvements in quality of life	■ Increased participation in social activities ■ Increased teacher and peer interaction in general education settings ■ Teacher and parent satisfaction ■ Progress toward full inclusion	■ Social activity log (weekly), Friendship Club schedule (peers) ■ Teacher progress notes (general education teacher) ■ Informal discussions, progress reports (parents, teachers) ■ Document inclusion plans and meeting notes (inclusion team)

Adapted from Meyer and Janney (1989).

APPENDIX D

Carl's (Abridged) Behavior Support Plan

Antecedent and setting-event modifications

- Provide a private, visual cue/signal to Carl prior to calling on him in group settings (e.g., stand in front of him and ask someone else a question first...then ask Carl a different question that he will likely be able to successfully answer).

- When feasible, break tasks involving reading into smaller pieces/chunks and ensure reading materials are at his instructional level.

- Pair verbal directions and written direction (e.g., have a student, not always Carl, state out loud what is expected).

- Increase use of proximity and positive reinforcement at onset of tasks that require Carl to read.

Alternative skills

General skills

- Improve Carl's reading skills as well as his organizational skills associated with academic tasks (particularly in science and social studies, which require the most reading).

Coping skills

- Teach Carl to momentarily close his eyes and take a deep breath when he feels frustrated or confused (e.g., when Carl feels confused with a social studies or science assignment); and then to raise his hand to ask for help or a break from the teacher.

Consequence interventions

Increase use of alternative skills

- Provide private verbal praise/ acknowledgment for (a) work effort, (b) improved reading and organizational skills, and (c) use of coping skills.

Reduce effectiveness of problem behavior

- Verbally redirect Carl to use his alternative skills (e.g., close eyes, take a deep breath, and raise hand to get help or request a break) and praise him for use of those same skills while requiring him to complete task/work.

Long-term supports

Maintenance/Generalization

- Reinforce Carl's use of the targeted alternative skills (a) over time and (b) across situations.

APPENDIX E

Resource Bibliography

Functional Assessment

Chandler, L. K., & Dahlquist, C. M. (2005). *Functional assessment: Strategies to prevent and remediate challenging behavior in school settings* (2nd ed.). Upper Saddle River, NJ: Pearson Education.

Crone, D. A., & Horner, R. H. (2003). *Building positive behavior support systems in schools: Functional behavioral assessment.* New York: Guilford Press.

Durand, V. M., & Crimmins, D. B. (1988). *The Motivation Assessment Scale (MAS) administration guide.* Topeka, KS: Monaco & Associates.

Foster-Johnson, L., & Dunlap, G. (1993). Using functional assessment to develop effective, individualized interventions for challenging behaviors. *Teaching Exceptional Children, 25,* 44–50.

Horner, R. H., & Carr, E. G. (1997). Behavioral support for students with severe disabilities: Functional assessment and comprehensive intervention. *Journal of Special Education, 31*(1), 84–104.

Knoster, T., & Llewellyn, G. (2007). Screening for an understanding of student problem behavior: An initial line of inquiry (3rd ed.). Bloomsburg: Bloomsburg University of Pennsylvania.

Knoster, T., & McCurdy, B. (2002). Best practices in functional behavioral assessment for designing individualized student programs. In A. Thomas & J. Grimes (Eds.), Best practices in school psychology (Vol. 4, pp. 1007–1028). Bethesda, MD: National Association of School Psychologists.

O'Neill, R. E., Horner, R. H., Albin, R. W., Sprague, J. R., Storey, K., & Newton, J. S. (1997). *Functional assessment and program development for problem behavior: A practical handbook* (2nd ed.). Pacific Grove, CA: Brookes/Cole Thomson Learning.

Touchette, P. E., MacDonald, R. F., & Langer, S. N. (1985). A scatterplot for identifying stimulus control of problem behavior. *Journal of Applied Behavior Analysis, 18,* 343–351.

Watson, T. S., & Steege, M. W. (2003). *Conducting school-based functional behavioral assessments: A practitioner's guide.* New York: Guilford Press.

Designing Individualized Support Plans

Bambara, L. M., & Kern, L. (Eds.). (2005). *Individualized supports for students with problem behavior: Designing positive behavior plans.* New York: Guilford Press.

Bambara, L. M., & Knoster, T. (1995). *Guidelines: Effective behavioral support.* Harrisburg: Pennsylvania Department of Education, Bureau of Special Education.

Bambara, L. M., Mitchell-Kvacky, N. A., & Iacobelli, S. (1994). Positive behavioral support for students with severe disabilities: An emerging multicomponent approach for addressing challenging behaviors. *School Psychology Review, 23,* 263–278.

Chafouleas, S., Riley-Tilman, T. C., & Sugai, G. (2007). *School-based behavioral assessment: Informing intervention and instruction.* New York: Guilford Press.

Crimmins, D., Farell, A. F., Smith, P. W., & Bailey, A. (2007). *Positive strategies for students with behavior problems.* Baltimore: Paul H. Brookes.

Hieneman, M., Childs, K., & Sergay, J. (2006). *Parenting with positive behavior support: A practical guide to resolving your child's difficult behavior.* Baltimore: Paul H. Brookes.

Horner, R. H., Albin, R. W., Sprague, J. R., & Todd, A. W. (2000). Positive behavior support. In M. E. Snell & F. Brown (Eds.), *Instruction of students with severe disabilities* (5th ed., pp. 207–243). Columbus, OH: Charles E. Merrill.

Jackson, L., & Panyan, M. V. (2001). *Positive behavioral support in the classroom: Principles and practices.* Baltimore: Paul H. Brookes.

Janney, R., & Snell, M. E. (2008). *Teachers' guides to inclusive practice: Behavioral support* (2nd ed.). Baltimore: Paul H. Brookes.

Meyer, L. H., & Evans, I. M. (1989). *Nonaversive intervention for behavior problems: A manual for home and community.* Baltimore: Paul H. Brookes.

Intervention Strategies

Agran, M., King-Sears, M. E., Wehmeyer, M. L., & Copeland, S. R. (2003). *Teachers' guides to inclusive practices: Student-directed learning.* Baltimore: Paul H. Brookes.

Bambara, L. M., & Koger, F. (1996). Opportunities for daily choice making. *Innovations* (No. 8). Washington, DC: American Association on Mental Retardation.

Carr, E. G., Levin, L., McConnachie, G., Carlson, J. I., Kemp, D. C., & Smith, C. E. (1994). *Communication based intervention for problem behavior: A year's guide for producing positive change.* Baltimore: Paul H. Brookes.

Colvin, G., & Sugai, G. (1988). Proactive strategies for managing social behavior problems: An instructional approach. *Education and Treatment of Children, 11,* 341–348.

Crone, D. A., Horner, R. H., & Hawken, L. S. (2004). *Responding to problem behavior in schools: The Behavior Education Program.* New York: Guilford Press.

Durand, V. M. (1990). *Severe behavior problems: A functional communication training approach.* New York: Guilford Press.

Janney, R., & Snell, M. E. (2006). *Social relationships and peer support: Teachers' guides to inclusive practice* (2nd ed.). Baltimore: Paul H. Brookes.

Teaming, Person-Centered Planning

Bambara, L. M., Nonnemacher, S., & Koger, F. (2005). Teaming. In L. M. Bambara & L. Kern (Eds.), *Individualized supports for students with problem behaviors* (pp. 71–106). New York: Guilford Press.

Holburn, S., Gordon, A., & Vietze, P. (2006). *Person-centered planning made easy: The picture method.* Baltimore: Paul. H. Brookes.

ncaid, D. (1996). Person-centered planning. In L. Koegel, G. Dunlap, & R. Koegel (Eds.), *Positive behavioral support: Including people with difficult behavior in the community* (pp. 439–465). Baltimore: Paul H. Brookes.

Sr l, M. E., & Janney, R. (2005). *Collaborative teaming: Teacher's guide to inclusive ractices* (2nd ed.). Baltimore: Paul H. Brookes.

Sch olwide PBS (SWPBS)

Cron D. A., & Horner, R. H. (2003). *Building positive behavior support systems in sch ols: Functional behavior assessment.* New York: Guilford Press.

Scott, T M., & Hunter, J. (2001). Initiating school-wide support systems: An a ministrator's guide to the process. *Beyond Behavior, 11,* 13–15.

Web Resources

Association for Positive Behavior Support. http://www.apbs.org

Center on Positive Behavior Intervention and Support (CPBIS), funded by the U.S. Department of Education Office of Special Education Programs (OSEP). http://www.pbis.org

Behavior Doctor! http://www.behaviordoctor.org

Online Academy, University of Kansas. http://uappbs.apbs.org

Research-Based References

Albin, R. W., Lucyshyn, J. M., Horner, R. H., & Flannery, K. B. (1996). Contextual fit for behavioral support plans. In L. Koegel, G. Dunlap, & R. Koegel (Eds.), *Positive behavioral support: Including people with difficult behavior in the community* (pp. 81–98). Baltimore: Paul H. Brookes.

Bambara, L. M., Nonnemacher, S., & Kern, L. (in press). Sustaining school-based individualized positive behavior supports: Perceived barriers and enablers. *Journal of Positive Behavior Interventions.*

Carr, E. G., Horner, R. H., Turnbull, A., Marquis, J. G., McLaughlin, D. M., McAtee, M. L., et al. (1999). *Positive behavior support for people with developmental disabilities: A research synthesis.* Washington, DC: American Association on Mental Retardation.

Clarke, S., Worcester, J., Dunlap, G., Murray, M., & Bradley-Klug, K. (2002). Using multiple measures to evaluate positive behavior support: A case example. *Journal of Positive Behavior Interventions, 4,* 131–145.

Durand, V. M. (1999). Functional communication training using assistive devices: Recruiting natural communities of reinforcement. *Journal of Applied Behavior Analysis, 32,* 247–267.

Durand, V. M., & Carr, E. G. (1991). Functional communication training to reduce challenging behavior: Maintenance and application in new settings. *Journal of Applied Behavior Analysis, 24,* 251–264.

Durand, V. M., & Merges, E. (2001). Functional communication training: A contemporary behavior analytic intervention for problem behaviors. *Focus on Autism and Other Developmental Disabilities, 16,* 110–119, 136.

Horner, R. H., Sugai, G., Todd, A. W., & Lewis-Palmer, T. (2005). Schoolwide positive behavior support. In L. M. Bambara & L. Kern (Eds.), *Individualized supports for students with problem behaviors: Designing positive behavior support plans* (pp. 359–390). New York: Guilford Press.

Kern, L., Choutka, C. M., & Sokol, N. (2002). Assessment-based antecedent interventions in natural settings to reduce challenging behaviors: An analysis of the literature. *Education and Treatment of Children, 25,* 113–130.

Kincaid, D., Knoster, T., Harrower, J. K., Shannon, P., & Bustamante, S. (2002). Measuring the impact of positive behavior support. *Journal of Positive Behavior Interventions, 2,* 109–117.

Meyer, L., & Janney, R. (1989). User friendly measures of meaningful outcomes: Evaluating behavioral interventions. *Journal of the Association for Persons with Severe Handicaps, 14,* 263–70.

Safran, S. P., & Oswald, K. (2003). Positive behavior supports: Can schools reshape disciplinary practices? *Exceptional Children, 69,* 361–373.

Turnbull, A., & Turnbull, R. (1999). Comprehensive lifestyle support for adults with challenging behavior: From rhetoric to reality. *Education and Training in Mental Retardation and Developmental Disabilities, 34,* 373–394.

NOTES

NOTES

NOTES